GW01081093

Indira Naidoo is one of Australia's most popular broadcasters. In a career spanning 25 years, she has hosted and reported for some of the country's most distinguished news and current affair programs, before more recently turning her journalistic attention to the issues of food, gardening and sustainability.

Indira's best-selling first book, *The Edible Balcony*, documented her adventures growing fruit and vegetables on her inner-city balcony and transforming them into delicious recipes. Her garden and recipes have featured on TV shows including *Gardening Australia*, *The Living Room* and *Better Homes and Gardens*. She has won awards for her food activism, promotion of sustainability and kitchen garden design. In 2014, Indira was the garden ambassador for Floriade Australia.

Hundreds of garden enthusiasts have joined Indira's urban garden tours of Sydney and her rooftop farm tours of New York City. For more information, go to theediblebalcony.com.au.

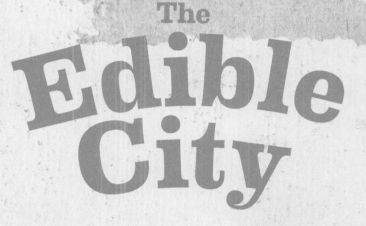

The Edible City

GROW · COOK · SHARE

Indira Naidoo

Photography by Alan Benson

LANTERN

an imprint of
PENGUIN BOOKS

Contents

Resistance is Fertile

As I've been travelling the length and breadth of this Great Southern Land, I've been witnessing a momentous change.

There's a quiet revolution rolling through our cities.

Urban armies are being mobilised across the country, in parks, along footpaths, in schools – even on rooftops. The troops in these battalions are difficult to detect.

They dress like civilians.

Instead of camouflage fatigues, you'll see gumboots.

Instead of wearing helmets, they wear sunhats.

Instead of carrying rifles, they carry rakes.

Instead of tanks, there are wheelbarrows.

And to mark their conquests they're not raising flags, they're raising garden beds.

These green guerrillas are on a mission to convert wasted urban land into productive spaces to grow food. If it's made from concrete or tarmac, it's on their hit list.

No footpath is safe. No road is protected. No roof is immune.

They want to liberate what lies beneath. And they won't rest until they have given life back to the soil and helped plants reclaim their rightful throne.

They know there will be resistance. But with missionary zeal, rules, by-laws, ordinances and courts will be quietly challenged and struck down. These liberators will install a New Green Order where vegetables will be free to grow throughout cities without fear.

I've watched and documented their silent insurgency with shock and awe.

These are their stories.

LOVE over HATE

The Wayside Chapel Rooftop Garden

You've got mail

The subject heading of the email was so improbable I almost hit the 'delete' button before reading its contents. It had been buried amongst some interesting correspondence from that day: 'Please transfer money into this Nigerian bank account to save my dying wife' . . . 'You've won $12 million in the Irish National Lottery!' . . . 'An invitation from David Wenham' . . .

Whoa! Back up a bit. David Wenham, the hunky Hollywood actor? I sat upright in my chair, slowly re-reading the name. D-A-V-I-D W-E-N-H-A-M. Yep. It read David Wenham all right. Surely it had to be spam. Diver Dan couldn't possibly know I existed, let alone be sending me an email. Still, I was intrigued. With a tremulous finger I clicked 'open'.

My initial scepticism seemed justified. The email was in fact not from David Wenham (below right) but from Reverend Graham Long (below left), the pastor at the Wayside Chapel, a Christian ministry in Kings Cross, Sydney. Like many local residents I had heard of the gregarious Reverend Long and held a deep admiration for the Wayside's work with the homeless and those struggling with drug addiction and mental health issues.

Reverend Long explained that the fifty-year-old Wayside Chapel and its buildings had recently undergone an extensive $8 million renovation. As part of the new sustainable redesign, a 200 square metre vegetable garden was being established on the rooftop, to grow fresh, nutritious food that would be served in the Wayside's cafe.

A vegetable garden on a rooftop? My gardening antennae began twitching. This email was becoming – to steal a line from another adventuress – curiouser and curiouser. I read on. 'Our Wayside ambassador David Wenham, the actor,' wrote the Reverend, 'recommended we approach you given the success of your book, *The Edible Balcony* . . . ' Ah! At last, the David Wenham connection was revealed.

The Edible Balcony charted my attempts to grow food on my thirteenth-floor balcony. It had been a successful if pretty nutty experiment. The Wayside concept, however, was decidedly wackier: an inner-city rooftop garden run by a homeless charity in one of the roughest neighbourhoods in the country.

The Reverend continued: 'David and I hoped you would consider joining the Wayside Chapel as one of our volunteer ambassadors and help promote and look after our vegetable garden. The garden is in a challenging location and will be largely run by the people we help, but no doubt a city gardener like yourself will relish the task. Would you be interested in running some gardening classes?'

David Wenham had recommended me for this role? Could he rise any higher in my affections? I thought dreamily. Indira-the-realist (yes, she does make an appearance occasionally) quickly made me re-focus and my eyes darted back to the Reverend's description of the garden as 'challenging'. That's an understatement, I thought.

While there was no denying the invitation was compelling, a thousand questions began racing through my mind. I did some quick calculations. At 200 square metres the Wayside garden would be one of the largest rooftop veggie patches in the country, if not *the* largest. And what about the location? How would food crops survive on a roof? I imagined there would be blustery winds, storms and searing heat to contend with, not to mention the marauding urban wildlife – vandalising cockatoos, possums and possibly rats.

Then there was the fact that the garden was to be run by staff and Wayside visitors (as the Wayside prefers calling its clients), many of whom would be homeless and some struggling with drug and mental health demons. Gardens need reliable

My gardening antennae began twitching.

attention. Who would water the plants, fertilise, harvest and care for them on a daily basis? There would be no or little budget for a dedicated professional horticulturalist. What would happen when the Wayside's social workers were busy with other duties or when visitors were waylaid by their illnesses? What's more, the Wayside relies upon charitable donations and grants. Even if we gathered a workable gardening team, would the funds be available to maintain such an extensive garden?

I'd also be kidding myself if I said I wasn't concerned about personal safety. Occasionally I would see a police car or an ambulance, sirens blaring, speeding towards the Wayside's Hughes Street address. Some damaged people do stupid things. Could I spend time in such a volatile and, at very rare moments, physically threatening environment? Working in television would seem like bingo night at the Harbord Diggers Club in comparison.

My husband, Mark, was predictably concerned when I told him about the Wayside invitation. 'Have you forgotten how difficult it was volunteering at the soup kitchen?' he asked, reminding me of my six-month stint making and serving sandwiches every Wednesday lunchtime at a local church. 'Many of the people suffered from schizophrenia and you found it pretty confronting at times.'

'I know,' I agreed, 'but ultimately it was a wonderfully rewarding experience. And don't I make a damned good sandwich now?' I quipped, trying to lighten the mood.

Mark's face remained stony.

'I do understand the challenges, Mark,' I said, trying another tack, 'but think about the difference a food garden would make to the troubled souls in our neighbourhood. They'd have a beautiful, relaxing green space away from the rough streets of the Cross. They'd develop some gardening and cooking skills – and maybe some professional qualifications to help them find work – and the food we'd grow would nourish and nurture them. We'd all share and learn and create a garden that could become a model for how communities can work together,' I intoned, channelling a poor-man's version of Martin Luther King's 'I Have a Dream' speech.

'But what if something happens to you up there?' Mark asked, voicing the question I was asking myself.

'I'm sure the staff will manage all that,' I said, trying to reassure myself as well. 'They're professionally trained. Everything will be fine.'

I could tell from Mark's expression that he wasn't convinced, but he knew it was pointless attempting to change my mind. After enduring five years of *The Edible Balcony*, Mark had become a hardened garden spouse.

Well, that was that then.

Reverend Graham Long and David Wenham were asking me to join a gardening mission that would test every part of my humanity.

Of course I had to say yes.

Falling by the Wayside

Morning with clouds. I shade my eyes and blink as I look up into the bright autumn sky. I can feel the crisp air on my face. The light is slowly dimming. A storm is brewing in the west. I do up my coat buttons, pull the collar over my ears and pick up my pace. I don't want to be late for my first meeting with Reverend Long.

Kings Cross is always a late riser, if it goes to bed at all. It usually begins the day nursing a mild hangover. At nine o'clock it's still groggy and unshaven until it tosses back that first macchiato. As the caffeine works its way through its tired body, its mood lifts and it's ready to tart itself up again for the long day and night ahead. It loves living on the edge. It's never going to die wondering.

Now that the morning rush hour is over the streets are quiet, almost mellow. I pass Rosie, who is settled in one of her favourite spots – on the street window-ledge of the Macleay on Manning design store. From here, in front of the Missoni blankets and Fornasetti plates, Rosie sits on her street throne and holds court with passers-by. She is wearing a chunky, woollen cable-knit men's jumper with fraying threads, several sizes too big. It's so bulky it looks like she's wearing a sheep. Her grey-white hair is wild. Of course she is engrossed in a book. I can't make out the title but it's probably Dostoyevsky or something equally high-brow. Rosie must be one of the most well-read people I've ever met. Living rough on the streets means she would have numerous tales to *fill* a few books as well. I say a quick 'hello' but keep moving.

I finally reach Hughes Street and make my way towards a huddle of buildings with a red brick and modern laser-cut metal facade. The Wayside Chapel doesn't look much like a church at all – which suits me. *I'm* not much of a religious person. Other than the word 'chapel' there are no church insignia, no spires, no crosses, no statues of saints. The Wayside is an independent arm of the Uniting Church and the building holds itself with that same sense of defiance. Despite its appearance, it's still very much a working church: Reverend Graham Long holds Sunday services in the chapel and conducts regular wedding and funeral services as well.

When I arrive, several people are milling around outside under the sprawling branches of a huge magnolia tree, which has somehow survived the recent redevelopment. Most of the Wayside's visitors are radiating a nervous energy that's palpable. Two gaunt men are sitting on the deck, huddled conspiratorially over a racing form guide. A young couple next to a pram with no baby look sad and despondent. An old man sits quietly, humming, gently rocking while rolling a cigarette. And nearer the entrance are two Aboriginal lads, laughing and teasing each other.

As I approach, some of the 'regulars' stop what they are doing to inspect the new arrival. I'm suddenly very self-conscious of my smart jacket and new leather boots. I wish I had worn an old pair of jeans and sneakers.

A woman inside the office spies me hovering and comes rushing out. 'Hello Indira!' she says, scooping me up in a warm embrace. 'We're so excited you're our new ambassador! I'm Laura. Come up to the roof and Graham will meet us there.' Laura Watts, the Wayside's marketing manager, has a wide-open optimism and generosity of spirit you sometimes see in highly spiritual people. I guess she's working in the right place. I like her immediately. She whisks me into the lift to the fourth floor and then up a flight of concrete stairs. At the top we go through a red door, which opens out onto the rooftop garden. Nothing could prepare me for this.

It's like being Alice in Wonderland. My

It's like being Alice in Wonderland.

eyes can't quite believe what they are seeing. Floating above the concrete and steel and gritty tarmac of the Cross is the most wondrous, improbable urban oasis I've ever seen.

The roof is laid out in a rough L-shape. Dotted along the western section on either side of a path is a series of large, waist-high black recycled plastic tubs, sitting on gravel and brimming with newly planted seedlings. To the right is a fenced-off area containing several photovoltaic solar panels and two 5000-litre rainwater tanks.

I am immediately struck by how secure the roof feels. I don't feel exposed or vulnerable. Sheltered by a towering ring of protective apartment blocks, it feels deceptively like being in a garden on the ground. The fences and northern concrete walls add to the illusion.

As I look around this leafy sanctuary, I have to remind myself we are still in the heart of Kings Cross. Other than the occasional strain of traffic drone, jackhammers and pedestrian chatter, the madding crowds five storeys below seem miles away.

'So you've seen our little garden then, have you?' says a voice from behind us. I turn around to see Reverend Graham Long beaming proudly. He shakes my hand with a firm grip, but all I really notice are his eyes. They are the eyes of a man who has seen the darkest side of humanity and somehow emerged a joyful warrior.

The long and winding road

When Graham Long joined the Wayside Chapel in 2004 as its general manager (later becoming its pastor and CEO), the inner-city icon was broke. Its buildings were derelict and the business was close to insolvent. Several court orders had its two main buildings condemned due to a lack of fire exits, and non-compliant fire doors and smoke seals.

If ever a miracle was needed it was then. When Graham asked his predecessor during his handover what plans he had to rescue the building, he replied, 'The Lord will provide'. 'Really?' said Graham. 'What's your Plan B?'

Graham relates the story with a gentle humour. He is a man of God and a man of the people. (He has worked as a prison counsellor and a postie, and has talked publicly about his brief suspension from the church for having an extramarital affair.) He describes himself as a 'tower of weakness'. But all I see is strength: the strength of Samson.

For half a century the Wayside has been welcoming people who have outstayed their welcome everywhere else: the homeless, the hungry, the haunted. It was founded in 1964 by the legendary Ted Noffs, who built it into an internationally recognised centre for compassion and acceptance. The Wayside provided the down and out with clothes, meals, addiction support and help with emergency accommodation. Most importantly, it was a place where people could come and not be judged.

In an era of extreme conservatism within churches, the Wayside shone like a beacon. Under Ted Noffs it also became a magnet for bohemian radicals. It held its own small theatre productions (some of which a young David Wenham attended with his father) and published *Cross Beat* poetry magazine and an ideas journal called *Logos.* With a new awakening about Australia's abysmal treatment of its Indigenous population, Ted supported Aboriginal activist Charlie Perkins' famous Freedom Ride in 1965. Much of the planning for this bus trip through country NSW and the media interviews it generated were conducted at the Wayside. In the 1967 referendum, a few years later, Australians voted to give Indigenous citizens protection under the constitution and to include them in the National Census.

But the campaigning took a toll on Ted's health and in 1987 Ted and the Wayside parted company. Ted died in 1995. His wife and son Wesley continued his work, forming the Ted Noffs Foundation, which to this day still delivers support to young people struggling with drugs and alcohol.

The Reverend Ray Richmond inherited Ted Noffs' well-loved church and, less appealingly, its empty coffers. How he kept the Wayside afloat during those years is still, as they say, 'a minor miracle'. Ray Richmond put the money worries aside and continued the centre's campaigning reputation. He opened 'The Tolerance Room', an illegal injecting centre in one of the Wayside's backrooms. He was arrested several times but kept the room open. He'd seen too many people die from overdoses and unsafe needle-sharing practices: the law would have to change, not the Wayside. His courageous acts of defiance eventually lead, in 2001, to the then New South Wales Premier Bob Carr setting up Australia's first medically supervised injecting centre just around the corner on Darlinghurst Road.

Graham knew immediately that he'd be the perfect fit for the Wayside. In his memoir *Love over Hate: Finding Life by the Wayside*, he writes, 'Some hunches are like a whisper in the ear and others are more like a shout. This hunch was more like a shout.' Yet, despite the serendipity of the appointment, he wondered if he'd been employed to bury the Wayside rather than preserve it. The Wayside might have been saving lives but it was struggling to save itself. It wasn't a safe place for anyone. The roof was leaking, its wooden structures were rotting, the carpets were mouldy. According to Graham, it was in such a dire state of disrepair that 'you could smell the Wayside before you could see it'.

While Graham's predecessor, Ray Richmond, didn't know how to pay for the renovations, he did know what he wanted – a new sustainable building that would utilise green technology. There would be solar heating, rainwater harvesting and a rooftop vegetable garden. Ray Richmond certainly dreamt big. The Wayside was having trouble finding money to 'change a light globe' and Ray wanted a state-of-the-art building that would cost at least $8 million.

This was the dream (and the nightmare) that Graham Long inherited. They say faith can move mountains. Well, in Graham's case, it had to do much more than that.

Rebuild it and they will come

Despite the Wayside's stellar reputation, government funding was hard to come by. Cost-cutting was the new mantra. Numerous pleas to the State Government fell on deaf ears and spirits ebbed.

Graham Long had no experience in business or in fundraising, but he quickly realised they were going to be central to the Wayside's salvation. He gradually installed a new board under chairman Ian Martin and asked him to target the 'big end of town' for donations and support.

Then in 2009, out of the blue, Premier Nathan Rees visited the Wayside and pledged a $2 million grant. The Wayside was back in business – all that was needed now was a Federal Government grant and the remainder of the $8 million target could be met with fundraising.

With Federal support not forthcoming, Graham galvanised his 'Inner Circle', a network of supporters who receive his weekly email about goings-on at the Wayside. Graham says in his memoirs that things went 'crazy' after that email:

'The next day the Wayside's plight was on page 3 of the *Sydney Morning Herald*. The morning after, we were featured in a live cross on Seven Network's *Sunrise* with David Koch. The following day we had a call from the office of Federal Minister Anthony Albanese, Minister for Regional Development and Local Government.'

For some weeks Wayside board member Colin Tate had been gently lobbying Prime Minister Kevin Rudd to come to the rescue. Inroads were made. Federal Minister Albanese personally dropped by to inspect the Wayside and hear about the redevelopment plans. And the very next day he returned to announce a $3 million grant. Graham was speechless. 'Albo' would never be forgotten for the critical role he played in saving the Wayside. The mountain was looking decidedly easier to move.

More acts of unbelievable support and generosity flowed in. Lucy and Malcolm Turnbull donated $250 000. Business entrepreneur and philanthropist Dick Smith deposited $300 000 into the Wayside's account on the same day he heard of their funding shortfall. And many others gave whatever they could spare, from $20 to $1000. Every dollar mattered. Soon the $8 million target had been reached. A combination of prayer and pragmatism had saved one of the country's most important institutions.

Sadly, after re-calculations there still wasn't enough to proceed with the ambitious rooftop garden. It was to have been an essential healing space for people who had no garden of their own, but its cost could not be covered. Another Inner Circle plea went out. Founder of the accommodation website Wotif, Graeme Wood, responded and donated $100 000, which with another $50 000 from other donations, went towards constructing the Wayside's long-held dream of a rooftop garden.

A community had done close to the impossible. It had rallied together to save its heart and soul – a place where the forsaken could be redeemed, where the unloved could be embraced, a place where there would be no 'us' and 'them'.

The mountain had been moved.

The architecture of happiness

Architect Tone Wheeler watched the unfolding drama with keen interest. Tone's architectural business, Environa Studio, specialises in green building design using the latest in sustainable technology. Tone had been helping the Wayside on a pro bono basis for ten years to come up with a design for its new headquarters. More than once, he reputedly dipped into his own pocket to pay for some hastily needed repairs to a leaky roof or damaged brickwork. (After years in the television industry I continue to be struck by the generosity of the people I meet in the Wayside's orbit.) Tone says he never doubted that a man of Graham Long's spirit and intellect would deliver him the budget he needed to transform the old Wayside.

Tone's passion for all things green is infectious. He describes himself as a 'hippy' and says his greying shaved head used to bounce with long red locks. When he was a student at the University of Sydney in the 1970s, he helped build the famous Autonomous House, a ground-breaking prototype for low-impact housing.

Tone took a '3L' approach to the new Wayside building: 'Long life, loose fit and low impact'. The main structure of the brick exterior and concrete columns, walls and floors will last for another century. At the same time, the fit-out and services are 'loosely fitted' to make repairs easier, reflecting Tone's practical motto of 'Use a spanner, not a hammer'. And all materials used were selected for their low environmental impact, from point of origin to manufacture and installation.

Water bills are kept to a minimum with the help of two 5000-litre rainwater tanks on the roof. There is no traditional air-conditioning or heating in the new section of the building. Warmth is generated passively from three gas-boosted solar thermal panels on the roof. This collected heat is then stored in the concrete floors. The building is cooled by two giant roof-mounted fans, a passive fresh air ventilation system, cross ventilation and mechanical fans.

This is a building that treads lightly on its patch of earth; a building that enhances the Wayside's work by providing a calm, nurturing space for it to continue its mission. But it is the bold rooftop garden that showcases Tone Wheeler's true design genius.

Sky high

The technology to build gardens on rooftops has been around since the fabled Hanging Gardens of Ancient Babylon in what is now modern-day Iraq. There is something quite magical about plants growing in the air – defying the very gravity that usually keeps them earth-bound. In a densely populated city where space on the ground is at a premium, rooftops are a free, under-utilised growing space. Not only that, green roofs insulate buildings, reducing heating and cooling costs. They also help prolong a roof's life by protecting the building against storm water damage.

And, wait, there's more! Planting on roofs (and in gardens generally) will reduce the harmful 'Heat Island Effect'. This phenomenon occurs when dense, heat-absorbent materials such as bitumen cause an increase in the overall average urban temperature. Plants counter this effect by cooling the area around them through the shade they provide. Tone Wheeler was thinking of all these environmental advantages when he incorporated a rooftop garden into his Wayside blueprint.

Tone worked with a structural engineer to ensure the weight of the roof material would be supported by the new building. Protecting the building from root damage and water leaks was also paramount. First a concrete slab was laid down so the garden would be completely separated from the rest of the building below. Next a waterproof membrane was applied. Then water retention and drainage matting, and finally a geo-textile layer, went on top to act as a filter, preventing fine soil particles from blocking the system. (Since the garden's completion, there has been only one minor leak, which was easily fixed. However, the automatic watering system has always been problematic, which means hand-watering with hoses and watering cans has been the garden's water delivery method. A tap in the garden is connected to the roof's rainwater tanks and when those tanks are running low there is also a mains water connection. While hand-watering improves the personal connection gardeners can have with a garden, the method can be inconsistent.)

To meet his 'loose fit' philosophy, Tone didn't want to install built-in garden beds. Instead he sourced 1 metre-high recycled plastic tubs that provide ample growing space but can be moved and replaced if required. They were lifted onto the roof in an elaborate exercise using a crane. The tubs sit on recycled gravel aggregate and the pathways curving between them are made from a clever recycled plastic/wood composite material known as 'modwood' decking. The planting medium was also important to get right. To keep extra weight on the roof to a minimum, the garden pots were first filled with a layer of lightweight mineral perlite and then topped with compost, potting mix and some mulch. And of course every garden needs a shed. A small room near the garden's entrance was converted into a storeroom for tools, gloves, hoses, watering cans, fertilisers, seeds and extra compost.

On Saturday, 19th May 2012, Tone's fifteen-year dream was opened to the public. The Wayside Chapel sat proudly glimmering in all its new glory. On an incredibly tight budget, Tone had created a structure of great beauty and integrity. Its use of high-tech green technology could have been cold and alienating; instead it welcomed people into its spaces with open arms. And to top it off, the Wayside now had a garden that would supply its cafe with fresh produce and, at the same time, provide its visitors with a much-needed green space in the rough and tumble of inner-city Sydney. This garden in the sky would touch the lives of all those who cared for it – including a narky former news presenter.

All that was needed now were the gardeners – and me!

First encounters

'This is the information you'll need to read should you encounter any blood spillages or syringe injuries, and we recommend you get a hepatitis B injection as well.' This is how my briefing session as a new Wayside ambassador and garden volunteer begins. Clearly this is going to be no ordinary garden.

As the head of the Wayside's Day to Day Living program, Wendy Suma (left) is responsible for managing services and people in an environment that can accelerate from calm to explosive in a microsecond. Now she also has a garden to contend with. *And* a well-meaning civilian who has little experience working alongside people with mental health issues or drug addictions. Wendy Suma could easily see me as a liability. I may only live two streets away but I could have come from another country. Life at the leafy end of gentrified Macleay Street in a comfortable apartment couldn't be more different from the rough street life of my fellow Wayside gardeners. I am beginning to realise the magnitude of what I've actually signed up for. The garden is going to be only part of the challenge.

Wendy Suma, on the other hand, is a hardened social warrior. She has spent time teaching English at the Klong Toey Slum in Bangkok and volunteering in the Kakuma Refugee Camp in Kenya. Her job at the Wayside is to deliver support and services while ensuring everyone is kept safe – including visitors, staff and volunteers. She lays down the ground rules for the rooftop and carefully watches my face. This is going to test my mettle.

'A staff member will be present at gardening classes at all times,' Wendy continues. 'If visitors are intoxicated they will not be allowed to join the weekly garden lesson that day.' Roofs are obviously dangerous places when you are high (so to speak). Wendy goes on with her list: 'Drugs are not permitted on the Wayside premises and will certainly not be tolerated on the rooftop. Do not carry any valuables with you and don't give anyone any money if they ask. It will be the beginning of a slippery slope. And don't give your personal address to any visitors and don't ask them to disclose any personal details to you.'

I nod wordlessly, taken aback by the rules of engagement. All of these 'boundaries' are going to make it exceptionally difficult to get to know my fellow gardeners in the way I am used to.

As I leave the meeting, the dizzying list of 'dos' and 'don'ts' has me reeling. How am I going to feel safe or comfortable in this foreign environment? How am I going to be of help when clearly I lack any social-work experience? And more importantly, how are we all going to work together to build a garden?

So to say I am slightly nervous about my first gardening workshop at the Wayside, given Wendy's briefing, would be an understatement. But when I arrive I realise I'm not the only one. Of course *my* presence in the group is something of an anomaly to everyone else. Some of the gardening group are old enough to remember me from my days on television, and my motivation for spending time in this comparatively unglamorous setting causes quite a buzz.

'You used to be that girl on the telly, didn't you?' says a man with a big open smile revealing several missing teeth.

'Yes. Yes, I did,' I say, surprised, in my ignorance, that I would encounter someone who watched the news, let alone any of the low-rating shows I worked on.

'Yeah. I remember you,' he says, inspecting my face a little too closely. 'I liked the way you covered the waterfront dispute in the late 1990s. Very balanced.'

This was my first interaction with Alan Claremont, one of the many gardeners who would touch my life.

The gardeners

Alan has since become one of the most deeply committed of all our Wayside gardeners, and I always look forward to our political discussions on the rooftop as the sun dips behind the city skyline. Despite his ongoing struggles with homelessness and depression, Alan is meticulous and dedicated, as nurturing as a doting grandfather. He told one of the many tour groups we have brought through the garden of his initial reaction when asked to help out: 'It made me laugh – they were asking someone who was suicidal to spend time on a rooftop,' he said, chuckling to himself. 'Very funny.' Alan has become so conscientious with his watering he has developed a naughty habit of also giving people on the street below a bit of a playful spray. Staff have had to put a stop to that.

The actress Claudia Karvan, one of the Wayside's other dedicated ambassadors, has joined our rooftop garden events several times. You just know she's mentally making notes when she hears these stories and I wonder if they will find their way into her next character or into the storyline of the next TV series she will produce. You couldn't invent a character like Alan.

Many of our gardeners are irregular and appear or disappear depending on their health and homeless status. It doesn't matter. Everyone is welcome – even those who just want to come up for a chat.

One of the regular irregulars is Lani, a gentle Aboriginal woman. She has lived rough on the streets of Kings Cross on and off since she was a teenager. Lani spent some of her childhood growing up on a farm and is very knowledgeable about plants and gardening, and teaches me many things about the Indigenous crops we grow.

A young man from the country joined us for a few months. He was living in a park nearby and was a natural in the garden. He'd studied horticulture at TAFE after he'd left prison and hoped volunteering at the Wayside would lead to a full-time gardening job with a council perhaps. Like so many other souls who dip in and out of the Wayside, he hasn't been seen for a while. I hope he is ok.

John has become the new garden stalwart. He is razor-sharp and keen to pick up some day-to-day living skills through working in the garden and preparing the produce in the Wayside's kitchen. He calls me Nidira. It's too endearing a moniker to correct him. One evening as we were watering in some new winter seedlings, John and I were discussing the importance of a carbon tax. He offered insights that had been missing from the national debate thus far. 'That's one of the few good things about being homeless, Nidira,' John said. 'You have a very small carbon footprint.'

Of course, gardening classes sometimes take a back seat to real-life dramas. We once halted a class so one of us could run down to the op shop to buy a belt to keep a visitor's pants from constantly falling down. Another class was suspended when someone began manically digging up the seedlings we had just carefully planted. And there have been times when working closely with others is too difficult for some and they snap and leave the rooftop mumbling expletives. But these are the exceptions. Most of our time spent

gardening on the roof is in happy harmony. After all, you can't stay angry for long when you're in a garden – as demonstrated by visitor Richard Geoff (Pee Wee), left.

Wendy, along with staff Bec McKenna, Jen Lee, Bill Suma and our volunteer horticulturalists Jon Kingston (pictured overleaf) and Lindsay Morrison, ensures everyone is assigned a job and supported and supervised. There are jobs for all levels – planting seeds, watering, harvesting, turning the compost bins, feeding the worm farms kitchen scraps from the cafe, or decanting the worm wee for fertiliser.

Over time, what grows in the garden has become secondary to what grows within us: a deeper understanding of each other and the daily hurdles many in our group face just to attend each week. Nowhere have I worked or socialised before, have I seen such a diverse cross-section of people come together for the common good.

For me, the hardest part of gardening class is when we're packing up our tools and saying, 'Goodbye, see you next week'. I wonder if I actually will. Many of my new friends will tonight be sleeping on a piece of cardboard in a park or in a doorway encountering a host of physical threats. As I wander back down Macleay Street returning to my safe world and comfortable bed, many of my fellow gardeners are heading to a decidedly unsafe world with only their wits to protect them. It's often only at the Wayside that they know no one will hurt them. Forcing people to sleep on the streets, in a country as wealthy as ours, can only be a stain on our national soul.

Alan articulates what the garden has grown to mean to him: 'The garden is a haven. A lot of hard work has gone into it and it's a great little place to get away and relax. The garden has come to life over the last couple of months. I enjoy seeing it grow and the little vegetables are great. I've had a bite of the odd lettuce leaf and they're full of flavour. I was homeless there for a while. I was living on the trains and I got myself into a lot of trouble and was in dire straits; my own fault. Wayside helped me. I became involved in the garden and I feel completely at home here.'

It is wonderful for people who have grown to expect so little from life to find beauty where they least expect it. Maybe when you are on a roof you really *are* closer to God?

The harvest

Many crops that grow well in the ground also grow well on a rooftop. Tone Wheeler says it was fortuitous, in hindsight, that one of his earlier designs for an extra floor on the building was knocked back: a rooftop on a sixth floor instead of the fifth would have been exposed to greater wind and heat stresses. A fierce gust can blow from the harbour along the ridge that runs through Potts Point along Macleay Street, and this wind tunnel can burn and desiccate many plants in its path. The Wayside roof is shielded by a protective phalanx of apartment blocks; I'm often surprised by how calm it is up there.

Everything in the garden is grown seasonally, using organic principles – usually from seeds we've collected from our last harvest. This reduces the need to buy plants and allows us to re-sow the best-tasting crops from the previous season. The garden's harvest is then used in meals served at the Wayside's

street-level cafe. Leafy greens, tomatoes, beetroots and herbs are most in demand for soups, sandwiches and frittatas. The delicious meals are not free but are heavily subsidised and available to the public as well throughout the day.

Jon, our incredibly dedicated horticulturalist, and Lindsay, our other volunteer garden instructor, have encouraged us to grow heritage and heirloom varieties of beans, peas, tomatoes and beetroot so we can produce crops that are better tasting and more prolific. Chioggia, an heirloom variety of candy-ringed beetroot, and purple-podded peas have been favourites.

Jon is the garden guru everyone wishes they had on tap. His knowledge is encyclopaedic and, after managing the James Street Reserve community garden in Redfern for many years, he is well versed in dealing with a variety of personalities and garden issues. Calm, gentle and always with a twinkle in his eyes, he is a natural teacher possessing the patience of Job. You know the garden is being looked after under his watch.

> Our garden is a reminder that we live in a community, not an 'economy'.

And Jon does this all for no money. Would many of our current political leaders understand the value of these transactions? I think not. Our garden is a constant reminder to me that we live in a community, not an 'economy'.

Our garden gurus ensure our productivity improves each season. One of our tubs is overflowing with a wild *fraise du bois* strawberry patch. These tiny, highly perfumed berries are our treat each week. Our gardeners become like children, excitedly searching through the dense leaf cover to find another sweet, juicy jewel.

We've planted several fruit-bearing trees to create some shade and protection for other edible shrubs. There are lemon, lime and fig trees, a lemon myrtle in our Indigenous beds, and a banana tree that has always struggled (the roof may be a little too exposed for it).

We grow a wide range of vegetables to reduce pest infestations and increase biodiversity and we've also planted beds of flowers, some edible, some insect attractants. Colourful bursts of nasturtiums, poppies, chamomile, daisies and hollyhocks bob between the lettuces and silverbeet. And since our garden is organic, we don't use any harmful sprays or insecti-cides. We control bad bugs with companion planting and the occasional jet of Neem Eco-Oil.

Keeping the cockatoos at bay has been less successful. One autumn the garden was ravaged by a gang of cockies that vandalised the garden for a week as we watched on helplessly. They didn't seem to eat much; these brutes just enjoyed snapping off branches, tramping on new seedlings and digging up roots. If you've ever faced off with a cocky you'd remember it. I made the mistake of treating one I saw settle down on a garden bed as though it was a bird. Never do this. Cockies are flying hyenas. This huge cocky puffed out its chest, extended its wings, looked me square in the eyes and let out a sound akin to a growl. I was petrified and reeled back a few steps. In the city he is at

the top of the food chain and no one was going to mess with him. Cockatoos are a protected species, so all you can do is wait until they get bored and move on. Hopefully our new scarecrow – dressed in Wayside op-shop finds – will deter future visits.

Watering is my favourite garden job. I enjoy watching the soft spray of water droplets catch the afternoon light as they bounce off the leaves. The plants drink it up thirstily. In those rare few moments I am in perfect union with sun, water, earth and nature. I look up and watch our little band of merry gardeners knee-deep in prunings or elbow-deep in manure. I notice no one is grumbling. These are the moments of true bliss.

The honey bees - supporting an important cause

A year after the garden was built, Wendy explored the possibility of installing a beehive on the roof. The bees would not only provide delicious honey for the Wayside Cafe but pollinate our crops at the same time. We had noticed how few bees were buzzing around in the garden, and after some research we soon discovered many food growers in the city had noticed a similar problem.

No one is keeping accurate figures but some reports say as much as 80 per cent of the wild bee populations of some countries, such as the US and Spain, could have already perished. It's been well documented how the phenomenon known as colony collapse disorder, together with the use of certain GMO crops and the application of agricultural pesticides known as neonicotinoids, may all be contributing to their destruction.

Neonicotinoids are some of the most-used pesticides in the world. The chemical is absorbed by the growing plant and becomes part of its structure, so an insect that ingests any part of the plant will get a nasty dose of neonicotinoid in its meal. These doses may not kill the insect immediately, but over time repeated uptake of the chemical will build up in the insect's system and paralyse its health, behaviour and reproductive success. Recently some EU countries imposed a ban on the use of neonicotinoids on flowering crops. These chemicals are also used here but so far the Australian government has resisted mounting pressure to follow suit.

There's a lot at stake. Sixty-five per cent of agricultural production in Australia depends on pollination by European honey bees. Thirty-five Australian industries are dependent on honey bee pollination for most of their production. And some industries (such as cherry, almond, apple and pear) are almost totally reliant on honey bees.

And there's another bee killer stalking our shores. The varroa mite has been decimating honey bee populations globally. It infiltrated New Zealand four years ago, leaving Australia the only varroa-free country in the world. Many farmers fear it's only a matter of time before the mite strikes our hives.

The Wayside built its reputation on supporting important causes. The plight of bees was going to be one of them.

Hive of activity

Former ABC TV investigative reporter John Millard (pictured overleaf), who has spent the past twelve years establishing beehives around Sydney, generously volunteered to help Wendy install and care for the Wayside's first hive of honey bees. He also began running monthly bee-keeping classes for the Wayside's homeless visitors, showing them how the bees make honey and how to extract and bottle the golden nectar.

John has set up beehives in the most unlikely of places, but the rooftop of a church-run homeless centre was a first. 'It's wonderful to see their [the Wayside's visitors]

fascination with the bees . . . to see their amazement as they take out a frame and see it dripping with honey,' he says. 'Honey is almost a daily part of what we eat, but how bees make it remains a mystery to most of us.'

I meet John on the Wayside roof to inspect the hive. The conditions are perfect: the day is warm, with not even a whisper of a breeze. John dons his spaceman-like protective beekeeper suit. I watch from a distance, safely behind the fence. I'm allergic to bee stings and, having been painfully stung as a small child, I have sadly developed an embarrassing phobia of these tiny creatures over the years. (If you want to see a grown woman completely lose her composure and start flailing her arms hysterically, scream-ing like a banshee, tell me there's a bee nearby.) I've only been stung once in the Wayside garden. It hurt, but the sting sac was removed quickly so I was all right. More impor-tantly I was probably targeted because I was wearing a strong perfume and the bee thought I was a flower! Spending more time around bees and watching them devotedly pollinate our plants has reduced my fear considerably. I just make sure I carry an Epi-pen with me in case I get an anaphylactic reaction to a sting. I don't want my phobia to stop me enjoying our bees. We learn our irrational fears; I hope I can unlearn mine.

John has been stung several times – it goes with the territory. He says beehives can readily co-exist with people in the city and the fear that bees will regularly sting is unfounded. 'We do have a duty of care, which we take seriously. The Wayside hive is in a fenced-off area on the roof, so no one is tempted to agitate the bees when I'm not there to supervise,' he says.

John believes it's never been more important to help expand and maintain healthy bee populations, especially in our cities: 'The reality is that bees are every-where, all the time . . . in our gardens and parks. They rarely trouble you and in exchange they do us this great philan-thropic service. But there are also native stingless bee varieties you can keep if you are really concerned.'

John slowly lifts the top of the white boxed hive and removes a frame of golden honeycomb. The bees are dozy and there's little need for his smoker to calm them down. Honey levels are high. When he holds the frame to the sun, I can see oozy pockets of syrup behind their wax caps.

The Wayside hive was hugely produc-tive in its first year. The queen bee was aggressive and a good egg-layer and the hive soon had 40 000 to 50 000 worker bees producing more than 30 kilograms

of honey a year. Most of this was used in meals prepared for the Wayside's cafe or as gifts for the Wayside's generous supporters.

Sadly, after a year the queen in the first hive died inexplicably, leading to the collapse and death of the entire hive. Our bees had possibly been struck down by the same mystery illness striking colonies globally. Everyone at the Wayside was devastated by the loss. Our bees had become our hard-working friends. It's easy to think of bees as robust creatures because they can have such a lethal sting. In fact, this incident made us realise how fragile and vulnerable they are to even slight environmental changes we are oblivious to. Bees are our reluctant canaries in a coal mine.

John sourced another nucleus, and a new hive soon replaced it and is now producing even more honey. Two years later the new Wayside bees are still thriving and you can often find them in the garden, particularly hovering around the flowering rosemary and calendulas. The Wayside bees forage for nectar and pollen in a 5-kilometre radius from the hive, taking in the nearby Sydney Royal Botanic Gardens and Centennial Park. The flowers they visit give the Wayside honey a distinctive local flavour and aroma. 'I think our bees mainly visit jacaranda and melaleuca flowers so the honey we get is very clear and sugary,' John says. 'And because our honey hasn't been heated and processed like commercial honeys, it has a much better flavour.'

Doug Purdie from the Urban Beehive has now taken over John's volunteer Wayside duties. Little maintenance of the hive is required and the benefits are enormous. 'I'm really excited that more and more city buildings are installing beehives on their rooftops,' says Doug. 'There are really no safety concerns for people if the hives are installed and managed correctly.' We've recently installed a hive of native sugarbag bees (*Tetragonula carbonaria*), which are stingless. Tiny and brownish black, they look more like a small fly than a bee. While they don't make enough honey for extraction, they still do an important job pollinating our plants.

As I've learnt, irrational fears are difficult to dispel because they are just that, irrational. If we are truly to protect these tiny creatures and the future of our diverse food supply, we should start accepting that we pose a greater risk to bees than they do to us. The Wayside garden is trying to do its bit. In doing so, it has become a haven, not just for people but for all the creatures who seek refuge in it.

Stairway to heaven

The Wayside rooftop garden has eclipsed everyone's ambitions. In 2013 it was the runner-up in *delicious.* magazine's ABC Local Radio Community award for the country's best community garden. It was also 'highly commended' in the *Green Lifestyle* magazine awards in the 'Garden: Community Group' section. The Wayside is now supplying Kylie Kwong's Potts Point restaurant, Billy Kwong, with honey for her famous pork buns. It doesn't get more local than that! And in 2014 Tone Wheeler's Wayside redesign won a NSW Architecture Award for Sustainable Architecture.

The satisfying sense of achievement and recognition these awards gave our gardeners was incredibly moving. When you're used to people ignoring you, moving away from you on the street, not making eye contact, to receive a form of national acknowledgement is overwhelming.

Like all great gardens, the Wayside garden has become more than a place to grow food. It is where we have forged friendships across the many divides; a place where we have shared ups and downs, successes and losses. We have built a lasting bond that can only come from caring about something outside of ourselves.

Nineteenth-century English poet Alfred Austin may have indeed been talking about our garden when he wrote: 'The glory of gardening: hands in the dirt, head in the sun, heart with nature. To nurture a garden is to feed not just the body, but the soul.'

How to:

KEEP NATIVE STINGLESS SUGARBAG BEES

Sugarbag bees (*Tetragonula carbonaria*) usually do not produce enough honey for extracting but they are important pollinators in the garden.

The bees prefer warm climates, from Sydney to northern Australia.

Hive boxes and nuclei are simple to install and can be posted to you if you live in the right climate. (Some councils even give them away free – check with your local council.)

Hives should be kept in a sheltered position out of the direct sun where temperatures do not exceed 40°C.

They don't need much space – even a small apartment balcony is sufficient.

There is no legal requirement to register hives of native bees in Australia.

You can find more information at aussiebee.com.au.

CARROTS

When to plant?
Hot humid climate: February–November
Hot dry climate: July–March
Cool temperate climate:
September–February

What to grow? Grow better from seed
and plant where you want them to grow.
Use organic seed and try the heirloom
varieties for better flavour.

Where to grow? In soil at least
30 cm deep. Thin out seedlings to
give plants room.

I like . . . sandy well-draining soil.

I don't like . . . rocky soil.

Feed me . . . go easy on the nitrogen-
based fertilisers to reduce leaf growth
and boost carrot size.

Give me a drink . . . I need a steady
supply of water.

RHUBARB

When to plant?
Hot humid climate: September
Hot dry climate: July–February
Cool temperate climate:
September–October

What to grow? From crown or seeds.

Where to grow? In pots or beds.

I like . . . cool winters and well-drained
soil enriched with animal manure.

I don't like . . . high temperatures or
high humidity.

Feed me . . . mulch annually in spring
with compost.

Give me a drink . . . regularly, but I will
rot at the base if over-watered.

LEMONS

When to plant?
Hot humid climate: March–November
Hot dry climate: Year-round but autumn is best
Cool temperate climate: April–June

What to grow? Grafted stock on hardy rootstock.

Where to grow? In full sun in a sheltered position. Will grow in all areas except locations that receive severe frosts.

I like . . . well-drained sandy loam soil.

I don't like . . . strong winds and harsh cold.

Feed me . . . with a well-balanced organic fertiliser in late February and citrus food in early spring.

Give me a drink . . . regularly, and if in a pot, every day when hot.

CUCUMBER

When to plant?
Hot humid climate: August–March
Hot dry climate: August–February
Cool temperate climate: September–February

What to grow? Bush, burpless or Lebanese varieties.

Where to grow? In pots or beds with a trellis to allow them to creep.

I like . . . good ventilation to reduce powdery mildew.

I don't like . . . growing in the same beds as tomatoes or potatoes.

Feed me . . . compost well when planting and then water in worm wee as fruit appear.

Give me a drink . . . often – I'm thirsty.

BEETROOT

When to plant?
Hot humid climate: Year-round
Hot dry climate: January–April; August–December
Cool temperate climate: January–April; September–December

What to grow? Seeds soaked overnight.

Where to grow? Garden or pots in well-drained fertile soil, with temperatures between 7°C and 25°C.

I like . . . plenty of sun.

I don't like . . . too much nitrogen, otherwise I'll produce too many leaves and small roots.

Feed me . . . a low-nitrogen liquid fertiliser such as kelp or fish emulsion.

Give me a drink . . . regularly.

Rosemary-infused gin fizz with borage flower ice-cubes

Serves 6

Herb-infused alcohol is a growing food trend at the moment. I first tried a rosemary-infused gin at The Westin Grand Central in New York last year. The hotel's bar manager, Zach Tirone, sources the rosemary from the hotel's rooftop vegetable garden on the 41st floor and leaves a few sprigs in a bottle of gin to infuse for about three days. It adds a subtle herbaceous note to cocktails. Needless to say I found it hard to stop at one . . . (hic!).

Borage flowers are sweet-tasting edible flowers that look very pretty suspended in ice-cubes. If you can't find them, try other unsprayed edible flowers, such as violets or pansies. Edible flowers are stocked in the fruit and veg section of some supermarkets or you can order them online from suppliers such as Darling Mills Farm (darlingmillsfarm.com.au).

12 borage flowers, calyx removed
1 cup (220 g) caster sugar
1 cup (250 ml) freshly squeezed lemon juice
soda water, to serve

ROSEMARY-INFUSED GIN

1 × 750 ml bottle gin
3 long sprigs rosemary

To make the rosemary-infused gin, place the rosemary in the gin bottle, ensuring it is completely submerged; you may have to tip a little of the gin out – or drink it! Leave to infuse for 3–5 days, tasting every day with a straw until you are happy with the intensity of flavour.

Fill a 12-hole ice-cube tray with water and place a borage flower in each compartment. Freeze overnight.

Place the sugar and 1 cup (250 ml) of water in a small saucepan over low heat. Heat until the sugar has dissolved and the mixture comes to the boil. Set aside to cool.

To assemble the fizz, pour 2 tablespoons of rosemary-infused gin into a glass. Add 2 tablespoons of lemon juice and 2 tablespoons of sugar syrup. Top with soda water and add a borage ice-cube or two.

Serve immediately.

Pesto pinwheels

Makes 40

The pesto from my first book, *The Edible Balcony*, has become one of its most popular recipes. I grow my own basil just so I can have a jar of fresh pesto in the fridge to add to whatever I am cooking – stuffed into chicken breasts, tossed through pasta, swirled over a pizza or, as in this recipe, spread over puff pastry for a quick canapé.

4 pre-rolled puff pastry sheets, thawed

⅓ cup (80 ml) milk

¼ cup (40 g) poppy seeds

PESTO

2 large handfuls basil leaves

1 large clove garlic, chopped

⅓ cup (50 g) pine nuts

½ cup (125 ml) olive oil

⅓ cup (25 g) finely grated parmesan

salt and freshly ground black pepper

To make the pesto, crush the basil, garlic and pine nuts using a mortar and pestle or a blender until a smooth paste forms. Slowly drizzle in the olive oil, stirring constantly (if using a blender, pour it in slowly with the motor running). Add the parmesan and season to taste with salt and pepper.

Lay out the pastry sheets and spread the pesto mixture evenly and thinly over the top, leaving one edge clear for sealing. Tightly roll up the sheets, starting away from the clear edge, then wet the clear edge with a little water and seal firmly. Leave in the fridge for 30 minutes.

Preheat the oven to 180°C fan forced (200°C conventional) and line a baking tray with baking paper.

Remove the pastry rolls from the fridge and slice them into 3 cm rounds. Arrange on the prepared tray and brush each slice with a little milk, then sprinkle with poppy seeds.

Bake for about 20 minutes or until golden. Serve immediately.

Coconut milk poached chicken salad with Wayside honey dressing

Serves 4 as a main or 8 as an entree

I'm always looking for ways to make my salad repertoire more interesting, and this tossed salad enlivened with Thai flavourings is a new favourite. The silky strips of chicken poached in coconut milk work beautifully with the cool and crunchy cucumber. Rather than waste the coconut poaching liquid, I use it to make coconut-flavoured rice, which can be served alongside.

2 skinless chicken breast fillets (about 300 g in total)

2 cups (500 ml) coconut milk

1 teaspoon ground turmeric

salt

½ cup (100 g) long-grain rice

2 lebanese cucumbers, halved lengthways, seeded and finely sliced into half-moons

4 red shallots, finely sliced

large handful mint leaves

large handful coriander leaves

DRESSING

½ cup (125 ml) fish sauce

2 tablespoons lime juice

3 teaspoons honey, preferably raw (I use Wayside honey)

2 teaspoons chilli powder

Place the chicken breasts in a small heavy-based saucepan and cover with the coconut milk. Add the turmeric. Bring to the boil over medium heat, then reduce the heat to low and cook for about 15 minutes or until the chicken is just cooked. Turn off the heat and remove the chicken, reserving the poaching liquid. Leave to cool, then shred the chicken with your fingers and add salt to taste. Set aside.

Return the coconut milk to the boil and add the rice with a pinch of salt. Cook for about 10 minutes until the liquid reduces and little pits form on the top of the rice. Turn off the heat, put on the lid and leave the rice to steam for about 10 minutes until cooked through and tender.

To make the dressing, place all the ingredients in a jar, then screw on the lid and shake to mix well.

In a bowl, combine the chicken, cucumber, shallot, mint and coriander, and toss through the dressing.

Serve the salad on a platter, with the rice alongside.

Slow-baked lamb shoulder with lemon, oregano and potatoes

Serves 4–6

There are few better ways to wow dinner guests than with slow-baked lamb. This version with its aromatic Mediterranean flavours always pleases. And best of all, the preparation and cooking can be done during the day so the domestic goddess in you has more time to relax with your guests.

1 tablespoon olive oil
1 lamb shoulder, on the bone
⅓ cup (80 ml) lemon juice
2 tablespoons chopped oregano
salt and freshly ground black pepper
1½ cups (375 ml) chicken stock
4–6 cloves garlic, peeled
8 large potatoes, skin on, halved

Preheat the oven to 160°C fan-forced (180°C conventional).

Heat the olive oil in a casserole over medium–high heat and brown the lamb shoulder well all over. Rub the lamb with the lemon juice and sprinkle with oregano, salt and pepper. Pour in the chicken stock and add the garlic and potatoes. Cover with foil and then the lid.

Bake for 3–4 hours, turning the lamb and potatoes every so often to ensure even browning and adding more stock or water if the liquid dries out. Remove the foil and lid and bake for a further 30 minutes until the meat is very tender and falling off the bone.

To serve, fork the lamb into chunks and spread on a platter with the potatoes, garlic and cooking juices.

Brussels sprouts with pancetta, pine nuts and currants

Serves 6 as a side

Few vegetables get as bad a rap as Brussels sprouts. It's only because, for most of us, we first experienced them boiled and sulphurous. This recipe, however, allows their texture and delicate taste to shine, especially when matched with their perfect companion, crispy pancetta.

1 tablespoon olive oil

4 strips pancetta, diced

400 g brussels sprouts, trimmed and halved

2 tablespoons chicken stock

½ cup (80 g) pine nuts

¼ cup (40 g) currants

4 cloves garlic, thinly sliced

1 teaspoon lemon juice

salt and freshly ground black pepper

Heat the olive oil in a heavy-based frying pan over medium heat, then add the pancetta and fry for about 5 minutes until crisp. Set aside.

In the same frying pan, fry the sprouts for 10–15 minutes over medium heat until they start to brown; add a little more olive oil if needed. Add a little chicken stock as the pan dries out. Add the pine nuts and currants, then the garlic and fry for 2 minutes. Add the cooked pancetta and lemon juice and toss through. Season with salt and pepper to taste, and serve.

Orange-glazed baby carrots with cumin, mint and labne

Serves 4 as a side

A few years ago, I had the amazing experience of staying at the Angsana Riads Resort in Marrakech, Morocco. The old city is a truly hypnotic place of exotic souks, high-walled alleys, turrets and hidden bath houses where locals enjoy the famous *hammam* massages. The food is very simple, with Asian, Arabic and African influences, and the aroma of freshly ground spices, especially cumin, is everywhere. Cumin seeds add a wonderful note to this baked carrot dish – versions of which appear on many Moroccan menus.

3 bunches baby carrots, trimmed

¼ cup (60 ml) freshly squeezed orange juice

2 tablespoons olive oil

2 teaspoons cumin seeds

1 tablespoon honey (I use Wayside honey)

salt and freshly ground black pepper

2 tablespoons sherry vinegar

large handful mint leaves

30 g labne (or make your own; see below)

lemon wedges, to serve

LABNE

1 kg Greek-style yoghurt

If you're making your own labne, place the yoghurt onto a clean muslin square, cheesecloth or tea towel. Tie the four corners of cloth together to form a hanging bag, then suspend it from a wooden spoon over a deep bowl. Leave to drain in the refrigerator for between 48 and 72 hours (the longer you leave it, the firmer the result). Spread the labne over bread, or roll it into 20 g balls, place in a sterilised jar and top with olive oil, then seal.

Preheat the oven to 200°C fan-forced (220°C conventional).

Toss the carrots in the orange juice. Transfer them to a baking dish and combine with the olive oil, cumin seeds, honey, and salt and pepper to taste. Roast for 20 minutes until just cooked and starting to caramelise.

Remove from the oven and deglaze with the sherry vinegar.

Scatter the mint and labne over the top. Season with pepper and serve with lemon wedges.

Sinful cheesecake brownies with pistachio pashmak

Makes 24

What do you get when you mix your favourite dessert with your favourite afternoon-tea indulgence? Suffice to say, if I was Catholic, I would have to head straight to confession after eating one of these brownies.

125 g unsalted butter, chopped
1 cup (220 g) dark brown sugar
125 g milk chocolate, chopped
3 eggs, lightly beaten
⅓ cup (50 g) plain flour
⅓ cup (35 g) cocoa powder
¼ teaspoon baking powder
250 g cream cheese, softened
¼ cup (55 g) caster sugar
1 teaspoon vanilla extract
1 tablespoon lemon juice
icing sugar, to dust
pistachio pashmak (Persian fairy floss), to decorate (optional)

Preheat the oven to 180°C fan-forced (200°C conventional). Lightly grease a 28 cm × 18 cm slice tin and line it with baking paper.

Melt the butter with the brown sugar in a heavy-based saucepan over low heat. When the sugar dissolves, add the chocolate and stir until melted. Take off the heat and leave to cool slightly, then whisk in the eggs until well combined.

Sift together the flour, cocoa and baking powder. Fold this into the chocolate mixture in the saucepan.

In a small bowl, whisk together the cream cheese, caster sugar, vanilla and lemon juice.

Pour the chocolate mixture into the prepared slice tin, then dollop over the cream cheese mixture. Swirl through, using a skewer.

Bake for 30–35 minutes; the sides should be set but the centre should still be gooey. Leave to cool completely in the tin, then slice into squares.

Serve with a dusting of icing sugar and a little pashmak on top, if you like.

Rosewater-poached rhubarb with vanilla ice-cream and crushed meringue

Serves 6

Every home garden should have some rhubarb growing in it. It can even thrive in a large pot if you only have a sunny balcony or courtyard. Any leftover poached rhubarb from this recipe can be spooned over your cereal for an indulgent breakfast the next morning.

VANILLA ICE-CREAM

1 cup (250 ml) full-fat milk

350 ml double cream

2 plump vanilla beans, split and seeds scraped

6 egg yolks

100 g caster sugar

pinch of salt

POACHED RHUBARB

120 g caster sugar

2 tablespoons rosewater

10 stems rhubarb, trimmed and cut into 4 cm pieces

MERINGUE

4 egg whites

125 g caster sugar

125 g icing sugar, sifted

To make the vanilla ice-cream, heat the milk and cream in a heavy-based saucepan over medium heat until almost boiling, then remove from the heat. Add the vanilla seeds and pods, and leave to infuse for 30 minutes.

Beat the egg yolks and sugar together until light and very fluffy. Remove the vanilla pods from the milk mixture, then whisk it into the egg yolk mixture.

Return the combined mixture to the saucepan and place over low heat. Add the salt. Stir constantly until the mixture thickens and coats the back of a spoon (don't let it boil or it will curdle). Remove the pan from the heat and strain the custard through a fine sieve into a bowl. Chill in the fridge for at least 4 hours, then churn in an ice-cream machine according to the manufacturer's instructions.

For the poached rhubarb, place the sugar, rosewater and 3 cups (750 ml) of water in a heavy-based saucepan and cook over low heat until the sugar dissolves. Add the rhubarb and cook gently until the rhubarb is just tender, about 10 minutes. Strain, reserving the syrup, and set the rhubarb aside in a bowl. Return the syrup to the pan over high heat and reduce by half, about 10 minutes. You should be left with about 1½ cups (375 ml) of syrup. Combine with the rhubarb and leave to cool.

For the meringue, preheat the oven to 110°C fan-forced (130°C conventional) and line a baking sheet with baking paper. In a bowl, whisk the egg whites with an electric mixer until they form soft peaks. Still whisking, shower in the caster sugar, a little at a time, and continue to whisk for about 10 minutes until shiny peaks form and the mixture holds firm. Shower in the icing sugar and fold through with a spatula. Drop tablespoons of the mixture onto the prepared baking sheet.

Bake for 1½ hours, then switch off the oven. Leave the meringues to cool in the oven for several hours or overnight.

To assemble, spoon some rhubarb and syrup onto each plate, add a scoop of vanilla ice-cream and crumble meringue over the top.

Lemon curd tartlets with lemon verbena

Makes 12

While most people are chocolate connoisseurs, I love the tang of citrus flavours in my desserts. And with the ready availability of pre-made pastry shells, this is a dessert that's also quick and fuss-free. You can serve these with a spoonful of creme fraiche on the side, if you wish.

12 pre-bought mini tartlet shells
lemon verbena leaves, to decorate
icing sugar, to dust

LEMON CURD
4 egg yolks
1 tablespoon finely grated lemon zest
½ cup (110 g) caster sugar
½ cup (125 ml) freshly squeezed lemon juice
180 g unsalted butter, chopped

To make the lemon curd, whisk the egg yolks, lemon zest and sugar in a heatproof bowl set over a saucepan of gently simmering water (making sure the bowl doesn't touch the water). Cook, stirring, until the sugar dissolves and the mixture becomes pale, about 15 minutes. Stir in the lemon juice and mix well. Add the butter, piece by piece, stirring well until all the butter has melted. Continue cooking until the mixture thickens enough to coat the back of a spoon; don't let the mixture boil. Leave to cool to room temperature.

Fill the tartlet shells with the lemon curd. Garnish with lemon verbena leaves and serve dusted with icing sugar.

Mesa Verde Restaurant Worm Farm

Decay and renewal

I'm beginning to realise that creating gardening spaces in cities is only limited by the imagination. Traditional veggie patches in backyards feel so predictable now, so lacking in daring. With a little light and water, edible plants will grow almost anywhere we will let them – on rooftops, on walls, on footpaths, even indoors. So why have we been so uninterested in exploring these possibilities?

Melbourne artist Richard Thomas (opposite) asked himself the same question. Richard has spent most of his life creating ecological art installations, using his hands to repurpose nature. He works with wood and rock, stone and metal. He's fascinated by the natural form and the everyday cycles of growth, decay and renewal. The redevelopment of Curtin House, one of Melbourne's most iconic buildings, has provided him with the canvas for his most daring project yet and has pushed the boundaries of urban agriculture.

Richard wondered if a restaurant could grow, cook and recycle its food all on site, reducing costs and harmful impacts on the environment. With his interest in decay, he started researching the role worms could play in this new urban model. The more he read, the stronger the idea became: he decided he would build the country's first rooftop worm farm on top of one of Melbourne's most glamorous restaurants.

Above the CBD

I'm standing on sun-bathed Swanston Street, shielding my eyes with my hand as I take in the full grandeur of Curtin House's six storeys. Of course, from street level there is no indication that on its rooftop a poo-producing factory bubbles away. I wonder how the scurrying pedestrians around me would react if I told them. Surprised? Repulsed? Report me to the police for accosting them? How did I become the 'stranger danger' my parents warned me about?

Anyway . . . I walk through the doors and instead of taking the lift, I walk the five flights of stairs to the Mesa Verde restaurant, where Richard Thomas is meeting me. The stairwell is dark and slightly musty and the concrete is cold under my feet. As the stairs circle up, I pass old plastered walls, pressed metal ceilings, wood panelling and torn cinema posters – all remnants of the building's rich, racy past.

When I eventually reach the sixth floor, the door near the stairs swings open and there is Richard to welcome me, beaming. He is wound up in a nervous coil of excited energy – after years of struggling to realise his dream he still can't quite believe someone wants to document his achievement in a book. Richard is lean and sinewy like the textured pieces of wood he often works with; his eyes flash with intelligence and curiosity. He updates me on his new city gardening venture as he leads me through the restaurant and to the rooftop walkway. As we step outside bright sunshine is streaming through a break in the low grey clouds, causing the garden's steel structure to pulse with an iridescent glow.

We walk up another short flight of steps, which leads to the garden. It's only from here, hovering above and amongst the skyscrapers of Melbourne's CBD, that I truly begin to appreciate Richard's vision. The surrounding buildings are dark and sombre, topped with ugly air-conditioning units, ventilation pipes and exhaust fans. Curtin House's rooftop sings in comparison. Its cage-like structure is open and vibrant and the greenery in the garden enlivens you. Everything is so tactile and textural, from the metal frames to the planter boxes to the beds of herbs and vegetables. The practical and the poetic in perfect synergy. To put a worm farm inside this floating jewel box is quite simply a bold stroke of genius.

Raising the Curtin

Richard Thomas couldn't have chosen a more unusual setting for his twenty-first century urban farm experiment. Curtin House is an imposing six-storey building, sitting majestically at 252 Swanston Street in the heart of the city, with trams zinging past its front doors and commuters noisily rushing along the footpath under its awning. It was built in 1922 during a short burst of prosperity wedged between two biting recessions. The economic optimism of the time inspired its architects to use the latest high-tech materials for its construction, which is how it became one of Australia's first concrete-reinforced buildings. Miraculously, its art-nouveau facade still retains almost all its original features.

In its ninety-year history, the building's fortunes have ebbed and flowed with the fortunes of Melbourne. Originally called The Tattersalls Club, it was renamed Curtin House after John Curtin, the Labor Prime Minister who steered Australia through the dark days of the Second World War. It became a very desirable address, housing an exclusive gentlemen's club, offices and ritzy shops and later even the short-lived headquarters of the Australian Communist Party. The following decades were not kind, however. Swanston Street became a red-light district populated by strip clubs, gambling dens and seedy bars. An 'R' rated adult cinema took up residence downstairs and Curtin House soon fell into neglect.

When restaurant developer Tim Peach stumbled upon the derelict site in 2000, he was determined it would not fall victim to an inner-city 'apartment conversion'. He wanted to transform the

site into a 'vertical laneway'. He envisioned Curtin House as an entertainment precinct with cafes, bars and cinemas: a place of books, music and ideas.

Tim and his business associates have spent the past fifteen years and millions of dollars restoring the *grand dame*. The whole building was rewired, fire escapes and sprinklers were installed, cracked parquetry floors were repaired and smashed lead-lighting windows were brought to life. One section of the roof was converted into a rooftop cinema; the award-winning Cookie restaurant and late-night bar and music venue The Toff of the Town also took up residence, as did a Kung Fu academy. And recently Tim opened his own restaurant, Mesa Verde, on the top floor.

Meanwhile Tim's long-time friend Richard Thomas began planting the seed for an even more daring venture to join the list of tenants. Richard's interest in art, nature and decay had expanded into a newfound fascination for worms. Compost worms to be exact, which don't

Curtin House would become the location for Australia's first rooftop worm farm.

burrow deep into the soil but live in the surface leaf matter on the forest floor. Richard had recently picked up the Australian franchise for the stylish new worm farm composting system 'The Hungry Bin', invented by New Zealander Ben Bell. Compact and streamlined, Hungry Bin worm farms can be incorporated into any size garden, which is where Richard saw their appeal. He convinced Tim that his new Mesa Verde restaurant could become an environmental showcase for urban food production and waste reduction by adding a worm farm and vegetable garden on its roof. Kitchen scraps from the restaurant could be composted in the worm bins and worm castings from the farm could be used to fertilise the veggies in the restaurant garden.

Tim is an entrepreneur who thinks big and Richard's concept was compelling. He gave it the green light. Richard was given his most challenging artist's commission to date. Not only would Curtin House be restored to its former glory but it would become the location for Australia's first rooftop worm farm.

High drama

Richard soon discovered that building his rooftop worm farm was going to be an exercise in endurance as much as anything else. Urban farmers need to be visionary and obsessive in equal measure. (I can certainly relate to the obsessive tag. Since beginning my edible balcony six years ago I have been encouraging others to convert their small spaces with an almost missionary zeal. Now, watching a floating garden take shape that leaves my handkerchief plot looking decidedly unambitious, I have a serious case of garden envy.)

Richard's drive was tireless. There were endless permits and DAs to apply for, council and fire regulations to comply with, and local businesses and neighbours who needed to be consulted. If this roof garden was ever going to be built, it would require a community of support and goodwill.

It was quickly apparent that the building's original walls would not have the strength to support a 30-tonne garden. Richard enlisted an engineering friend who specialised in steel fabrication. He began designing a bespoke steel platform and support structures that could take the weight bearing of a vegetable garden, worm bins and a cool room for the restaurant.

Richard says it was like constructing a platform from a 'giant meccano set'. It was so intricate and painstaking and it all had to be delicately juggled into place dozens of metres in the air. When the steel structure was finally complete, Richard began work constructing the garden and worm farm.

As an artist and designer he wanted the space to be as beautiful as it was practical. And given his background working with trees, wood had to be a feature. He sourced Tasmanian oak floorboard offcuts to build his planter boxes, as they would be sturdy and weather-resistant, and used a combination of wood and steel fencing for his trellis system. The five large worm bins, processing about 10 kilograms of kitchen waste every day, would sit under the garden next to the cool room.

But completing this engineering and architectural feat wasn't enough for Richard. The ecological artist in him wanted to add a 'living sculpture' to the garden that would wow rooftop cinema-goers and restaurant patrons. He wanted to create an ecological emblem.

His search took him to the Grampian National Park, 234 kilometres west of Melbourne. Here in a remnant forest he sourced a 500-year-old red gum log that carried its years in its weathered lines and muted hues. Only problem was it weighed a tonne. Literally.

Richard wasn't daunted. With National Park approval, the log was trucked back and the laneway and cafe behind Curtin House were closed for several hours as a crane lifted it onto a specially built steel platform. The ancient log defied its weight and seemed to levitate over its new urban landscape. Richard had brought nature to the city. And with their elaborate new urban home completed, it was time to introduce 5000 wriggling residents to their compost haven.

Squirm like a worm

A rooftop in the middle of Melbourne's CBD is an unusual location to contemplate decay. Unusual, and apt at the same time. Everything around us is in a constant state of decay (yes, I know what you're thinking: *Just look in the mirror, Indira*). Most of us move too fast to notice but it is happening outside us, on us and deep within us. We share our bodies with millions of organisms. A microflora of bacteria, fungi, viruses and protozoas help us maintain a healthy digestive system and protect us from skin-borne attack. In fact microbiologists have discovered nine out of ten cells in our body belong not to us but to these microbial species, and that 99 per cent of the DNA we carry around belongs to these microscopic critters.

When you understand the important role of this decomposing world, the humble worm sits like a king on a throne. They may do their work out of sight, but what they create becomes the foundation of all life. Composting worms in particular (not regular garden worms) help decompose organic matter, which then becomes soil that supports plant life, and the animals – like us – that feed on them. The by-product of the worm's composting process is a nutrient-rich poo or worm castings (vermicast) and worm wee or juice that give plants a pseudoephedrine-like boost. These nutrients contain trace elements that build a plant's immune system and lead to stronger growth and higher yields.

Composting worms eat more organic matter than regular earthworms and multiply

faster, which is why most worm farm systems use them. They are big and long and come in red, blue and tiger varieties. They have hearty appetites, making them perfect as food-waste consumers. A compost worm – like me if I'm allowed to – can eat its weight in food every day.

Richard's worms still may have more food waste than they can go through. Even a waste-mindful restaurant such as Mesa Verde throws away an enormous amount. In fact, in most cities, food waste makes up almost half of the waste stream. Australians throw away 4 million tonnes of perfectly edible food every year. Food waste is expensive to collect, transport and dispose of. And when organic waste breaks down in a landfill, it generates methane, a powerful greenhouse gas. Worse still, once that organic waste is buried, all the nutrients contained in food scraps are then lost to the environment and cannot be reused.

One of the solutions is to compost organic waste on-site, reducing handling and transport costs, and preventing valuable nutrients from being lost. A worm farm is one of the best ways of breaking this destructive environmental cycle. Richard wanted his rooftop worm farm to 'close the loop'. The restaurant's food waste would be fed to the worms, the fertilisers they produced would feed the vegetable garden, and produce from the garden would be used in the restaurant to feed customers. Zero food miles.

Many people are familiar with the black tray-style worm farm, which allows you to put food scraps in the top tray and remove worm castings from the bottom and decant worm wee from the tap. The Hungry Bin system is a little different. The first thing you notice is its striking design. The sleek bins are green and streamlined for the eco-stylish. They have a firm-fitting

hinged lid to keep insects out and taper to a tray where worm castings can be collected. Their compact shape means they are suitable for small spaces such as balconies and courtyards. Putting the whole system on wheels makes the bin easier to move or relocate.

Richard wanted his worm farm to demonstrate the efficiency and domestic application of the bins. In a cool, protected shed just under the garden, he installed five bins to begin with. They were soon filled with 5000 worms chomping through 10 kilograms of restaurant waste a day. Richard's next challenge was keeping his worms happy and healthy high in the sky.

Happy as Larry

Richard flips open one of his worm bins and scoops up a huge handful of wriggling worms. I'm expecting the bin to smell like rotting food but it actually gives off a sweet, earthy aroma similar to the damp floor of a rainforest. This, Richard explains, shows the worms are happy and the organic material in the bin is decomposing correctly. A bad smell indicates all is not well.

Richard encourages me to scoop up a wriggling ball of worms in my hand. I do so hesitantly. The worms are cold and clammy and tickle as they squirm and try to hide from the light. I fight the urge to drop them back in the bin. What little kid hasn't been frightened unexpectedly by a friend dangling a worm in their face? I'm surprised how

strong the memory is. To Richard, I look the picture of composure. Inside, I've reverted to that little girl in pigtails being terrorised by a hapless worm held hostage by a grotty pint-sized tormentor. It's hard pretending to be a grown-up, isn't it?

Yet, despite their reputation, worms are actually incredibly clean. They have no known diseases and their digestive system destroys pathogens. The job they do cannot be compared to anything else. I am in awe of worms. If everyone had a worm farm our compostable garbage would be reduced by 1 tonne per person per year. That's something to munch on, isn't it?

Richard recommends you take the following steps to ensure your wonderful worms are kept happy and healthy. First of all, your worm bins should be located in a cool, dry place out of any direct hot afternoon sun. To begin setting up your farm, half-fill the bin with soil and compost and add about 1000 compost worms. (These can be sent in the post from the worm farm company or sourced from nurseries and hardware stores.) Cover the soil with a layer of damp newspaper or old carpet to keep the worms moist – but whatever you do, don't over-water them or they will drown.

After letting your worms settle into their bedding material for a week or so, you can give them their first feed. Worms like a varied diet and you can use most food scraps – odd bits of lettuce, banana peels and old bread. Worms also love coffee grounds and tea bags and you can even throw in dust and dog hair from your vacuum-cleaner bags, along with shredded newspaper and cardboard as well. Bear in mind, however, that worms are basically vegans and they don't like meat or dairy products. You should also refrain from adding too many onions or citrus fruits, as they find them acidic. Avoid garden clippings that are too tough or big, as it will take worms just too long to chomp through them. The smaller the food scraps, the quicker the worms can break them down.

If your worm farm gets too dry or attracts ants, Richard recommends adding some vegetable matter and sprinkling it with water. If the worm farm starts attracting vinegar flies, it means it has become too acidic. Don't worry – this is easily rebalanced with a sprinkling of lime and a gentle toss with a stick.

After about four or five months, a thick layer of worm castings will have built up at the bottom of the bin. You can remove this and add it to your garden. Just remember it's potent stuff and a small piece is enough to place around one shrub. If there are some worms in your castings, leave them in the sunlight and they will burrow down, allowing you to scrape off the top layer. Worm juice from the bin can also be collected from the bottom tray, diluted one part to nine with water and sprinkled over the garden.

Sky garden

Within months Mesa Verde's worms began producing litres of plant fertiliser. Richard Thomas now waters the nutrient-rich worm wee into his rooftop vegetable garden to help fortify the plants. The worm juice is rich in beneficial bacteria, minerals such as calcium, nitrates and potassium, and trace elements such as zinc and magnesium. Now that's a boost juice!

While Richard is not a trained horti-culturalist, as an artist he has worked intimately enough with plants to realise that wind and harsh sun are their natural enemies. Sadly his grand plan for an espaliered lemon and lime fence was abandoned after he eventually accepted citrus would never adapt to the windy conditions. He also underestimated the problem birds would be. As soon as any seeds were cast, in would fly marauding sparrows to peck away at the germinating delicacies. They were particularly fond of radish seedlings. 'It was so frustrating,' says Richard, 'that I began seeing the birds as vermin, not as nature's creatures.' Eventually the only solution to their attacks was to use a fabric bird netting that still allowed pollinators to get through.

After two years of experimenting, Richard has settled on a range of herbs, greens, tomatoes, beetroots, chillies and peppers. He says the kiwi fruit are doing well, creeping over the trellis, and the grape vines are currently going 'berserk'.

While the restaurant goes through more fresh produce than Richard can grow in his tiny sky patch, every dish contains something from the garden. There are always fresh herbs that Mesa Verde's chef and co-owner, Kathy Reed, can throw into her meso-American dishes. Her marinated roof-garden beetroot salad with watermelon, pomegranate and radish sprouts has become a signature dish. Then there are her stuffed tortillas, baked chicken and array of dips. Even the bar uses tiny fronds from the garden's 'cola' shrubs – yes, as in coca-cola – to flavour a range of its cocktails. (I've downed several. I can vouch for their deliciousness.)

Worm wisdom

In 2013 Mesa Verde was awarded the City of Melbourne's Business 3000 Best Sustainable Business award for its environmental achievements. Judges were impressed by its food production, composting system and rainwater harvesting tank, which will be reticulating water into the garden soon.

Visitors to the Mesa Verde restaurant and rooftop cinema now walk past Richard Thomas' wondrous floating green oasis and can't help but be bewitched by its charms. It's often booked for celebration dinners and corporate workshops. Richard, Tim Peach, Kathy Reed and the team at Mesa Verde have created what many believed was not possible: a restaurant in the heart of the CBD, six floors in the air, with its own worm farm and kitchen garden. They have proved that with a little imagination and a lot of determination, reducing your carbon footprint can be rewarding and beautiful, and good for business.

How to:

START A WORM FARM

Keep your worm farm in a cool, dry spot in your garden or balcony away from the sun.

You can purchase your worms with your farm (try hungrybin.co.nz) or from a reputable nursery or hardware store, or in the mail.

Worms are basically vegans, so no meat or cheese please. Keep acidic veggies like onions and tomatoes to a minimum. Worms like newspaper, crushed eggshells, coffee grounds and teabags.

You can sprinkle lime, wood ash or dolomite on the worm farm every few weeks to keep the pH levels at optimum.

Make sure the farm is kept moist with a light sprinkling of water. Keep it out of the rain, though, or your worms will drown.

Keep the lid closed to stop insects and vermin getting in.

Depending on the worm farm system you have selected, worm juice and castings can be collected after a few months and added to your garden.

COLA

When to plant?
Hot humid climate: June
Hot dry climate: June–July
Cool temperate climate: September–March

What to grow? Seed, seedling or cutting.

Where to grow? In beds or pots.

I like . . . warm sunny spots.

I don't like . . . shade.

Feed me . . . worm juice diluted in water.

Give me a drink . . . regularly.

DILL

When to plant?
Hot humid climate: June
Hot dry climate: June–July
Cool temperate climate: September–October

What to grow? Grows well from seed.

Where to grow? In garden or deep pots. Will grow up to 1 metre; may need staking.

I like . . . basking in the sun, like most herbs.

I don't like . . . frosts.

Feed me . . . I thrive in rich soil, with an occasional liquid feed.

Give me a drink . . . regularly.

WITLOF (BELGIAN ENDIVE, CHICORY)

When to plant?
Hot humid climate: April–June
Hot dry climate: June–July
Cool temperate climate: September–November

What to grow? Seeds.

Where to grow? Direct seed into pots. Move into shade after four months so leaves stay white and retain their flavour.

I like . . . cool temperatures.

I don't like . . . strong sun.

Feed me . . . with a mixed fertiliser (NKP).

Give me a drink . . . regularly.

ICEBERG LETTUCE

When to plant?
Hot humid climate: April–June
Hot dry climate: March–October
Cool temperate climate: Year-round

What to grow? From seed or seedling.

Where to grow? In partially shady spots.

I like . . . well-draining soil with lots of organic matter.

I don't like . . . the heat.

Feed me . . . every fortnight with liquid fertiliser.

Give me a drink . . . regularly.

RADICCHIO

When to plant?
Hot humid climate: April–June
Hot dry climate: June–July
Cool temperate climate: September–November

What to grow? From seed.

Where to grow? In beds or containers.

I like . . . rich fertile soil.

I don't like . . . caterpillars and slugs.

Feed me . . . low-nitrogen fertiliser, such as liquid seaweed.

Give me a drink . . . often but lightly.

EDIBLE FLOWERS

When to plant?
Hot humid climate: Year-round
Hot dry climate: September–April
Cool temperate climate: Can grow throughout most of the year.
Pansies particularly like cold weather.

What to grow? Nasturtiums, pineapple sage, marigolds,
pansies, calendula.

Where to grow? Direct sow into garden or in pots. Harvest early
or late in the day. Remove stamens and styles (reproductive parts),
which may be bitter, and remove any pollen before eating as it can
trigger hay-fever or asthma in sufferers.

I like . . . good sun.

I don't like . . . pesticides.

Feed me . . . once a fortnight with a liquid fertiliser.

Give me a drink . . . regularly.

Iceberg lettuce wedges with salad cream

Serves 4 as an entree or a side

I'm so glad that, like chardonnay, iceberg lettuce is in vogue again with the foodinistas. It's my favourite lettuce. With its great crunch and cool mild flavour, it can carry a salad all on its own. I serve this as an entree or as a side with a main course. Ice, ice, baby . . .

1 iceberg lettuce, chilled

chopped chives, to garnish

SALAD CREAM

¼ cup (80 ml) well-shaken cultured buttermilk

2 tablespoons mayonnaise

1 teaspoon white vinegar

salt and freshly ground black pepper

To make the salad cream, whisk all the ingredients in a bowl until well combined. Season to taste.

Slice the lettuce into wedges. Drizzle the salad cream over the top sprinkle with chopped chives. Serve immediately.

Quail eggs with dukkah

Serves 8 as an entree

I'm currently tossing around the idea of getting a few quail for my edible balcony.
They can be kept legally in cages and can lay up to 10 eggs each a week.
I daydream about feeding them worms from my worm farm to supplement
their diet and using their manure in my garden pots. My husband, Mark,
says I'm taking this whole balcony farm thing way too far . . .

8 quail eggs
1 teaspoon white vinegar
100 g dukkah
salt

Boil the quail eggs for 2½ minutes in a small saucepan of boiling water with vinegar
added (the vinegar will make the shells easier to peel). A 2½ minute boil will result
in an egg with a slightly runny yolk but set white. Cook longer if desired.

Drain, then peel the eggs carefully.

Place a tablespoon of dukkah on each small serving plate, create a small indentation
with the back of a spoon and place a quail egg on top. Alternatively, sprinkle the dukkah
over a platter and arrange the eggs on top, rolling them a little to coat. Sprinkle with
salt and serve immediately.

Smoked trout with witlof and radicchio

Serves 8 as an entree

I love nibbles. I could easily just graze on a selection of tasty morsels for dinner instead of sitting down to a full meal. The boat shape of witlof leaves provides a perfect vessel for a range of fillings – particularly ones with a creamy texture to balance out the tartness of the leaves. Throw away the crackers, I say, and embrace witlof!

¼ cup (60 g) creme fraiche
1 tablespoon mayonnaise
2 tablespoons capers, rinsed and chopped
1 tablespoon lemon juice
1 tablespoon lemon thyme leaves
2 tablespoons chopped dill, plus sprigs to garnish
275 g smoked ocean trout
salt and freshly ground black pepper
2 witlof (endives), trimmed and leaves separated
2 radicchio, trimmed and leaves separated

In a bowl, combine the creme fraiche, mayonnaise, capers, lemon juice, lemon thyme and chopped dill.

Remove the skin and any bones from the ocean trout and flake it into the creme fraiche mixture. Season to taste; the trout is quite salty so you won't need to add much more.

Spoon the smoked trout filling into the individual witlof and radicchio leaves and top with dill. Serve immediately.

Edible flower salad

Serves 6 as a side

This salad is almost too pretty to eat. Do make sure the flowers have not been sprayed with harmful pesticides or chemicals. If I'm running low on my balcony supplies, I source my edible flowers from Darling Mills Farm in New South Wales (darlingmillsfarm.com.au). Check the website for local deliveries and stockists.

1 radicchio, leaves separated
2 large handfuls mixed lettuce leaves
1 large handful beetroot leaves
4 handfuls edible flowers (borage, pansies, marigolds, sweet peas, violets)

DRESSING

1 teaspoon dijon mustard
1 teaspoon minced garlic
¼ cup (60 ml) herb vinegar
½ cup (125 ml) extra virgin olive oil
salt and freshly ground black pepper

Arrange the radicchio, lettuce and beetroot leaves in a serving dish.

Place all the dressing ingredients in a small jar, screw on the lid and shake to combine.

Pour the dressing over the salad and sprinkle with the edible flowers.
Serve immediately.

Tagliata with salsa verde
Serves 4 as an entree

We can learn a lot from the relaxed entertaining style of the Italians. These beautiful sirloin steaks—sliced, arranged on a central wooden platter and drizzled with salsa verde—are the epitome of crowd-pleasing simplicity.

2 tablespoons olive oil

salt and freshly ground black pepper

2 sirloin steaks (about 400 g each), at room temperature

rocket salad, to serve

SALSA VERDE

4 anchovy fillets

1½ tablespoons capers, rinsed

2 cloves garlic, crushed

1½ tablespoons dijon mustard

1½ tablespoons sherry vinegar or red-wine vinegar

2 large handfuls flat-leaf parsley leaves

100 ml extra virgin olive oil

salt and freshly ground black pepper

For the salsa verde, place all the ingredients except for the olive oil in a food processor. Process while gradually pouring in the oil until combined. Season to taste. Set aside.

Heat a char-grill pan over high heat until almost smoking. Rub the olive oil and salt and pepper over the steaks and cook for 4 minutes on each side for medium–rare.

Pour some of the salsa verde onto a platter and place the cooked steaks on top to rest for 5–7 minutes.

Slice the steak diagonally into 2 cm strips. Serve with extra salsa verde on the side.

Serve with a rocket salad.

Leek, thyme and cheddar brioche

Serves 8

If you're someone who's been a little scared of making breads in the past, this is the recipe for you. This brioche is beautifully simple, and has a rich, buttery texture. Play around with your own topping combo – throw on some onions, or red capsicum or even some thinly sliced mushrooms with feta or goat's cheese.

150 ml lukewarm milk

1 × 7 g sachet yeast

2 tablespoons caster sugar

1 egg, beaten

100 g butter, at room temperature, chopped

½ cup (140 g) natural yoghurt

3 cups (450 g) plain flour

160 g sharp cheddar, grated

⅓ cup (80 ml) olive oil

½ leek (white and some green), finely shredded

4 cloves garlic, thinly sliced

4 sprigs thyme, leaves picked, plus extra sprigs to garnish

salt and freshly ground black pepper

Mix the milk, yeast and sugar in a large bowl and leave in a warm place for 4–5 minutes until the mixture froths. Add the egg, butter and yoghurt to the yeast mixture, then add the flour and half the cheese. Mix well.

Knead the dough for 5 minutes in the bowl until soft. Cover the bowl with plastic film and leave in a warm place for 45 minutes to 1 hour until doubled in size.

Preheat the oven to 180°C fan-forced (200°C conventional). Line and butter a 30 cm × 20 cm × 3 cm slice tin.

Add half the olive oil to a frying pan and place over medium heat. Add the leek, garlic and thyme and fry for 10 minutes or until very soft. Season with salt and pepper. Set aside.

When the dough has risen, knock out the air with your fist and shape it into a rectangle to fit the tin. Place the dough in the tin and make a few deep indentations with your fingers. Spread with the leek mixture, pushing it into the indentations. Sprinkle with the remaining cheese and olive oil.

Bake for 35-40 minutes or until the crust sounds hollow when rapped with your knuckle.

Turn onto a rack to cool. Serve warm or at room temperature, garnished with thyme sprigs.

Fig, buffalo mozzarella, pomegranate and mint salad

Serves 6 as an entree or side

To me, a great salad is all about getting the balance of flavours and textures just right. You want sharpness and sweetness, creaminess and crunch. This salad ticks all the boxes.

4 figs, torn
110 g buffalo mozzarella
1 pomegranate, halved
large handful mint leaves

DRESSING

1 tablespoon pomegranate molasses
⅓ cup (80 ml) olive oil
1 tablespoon lemon juice
salt and freshly ground black pepper

To make the dressing, mix all the pomegranate molasses, olive oil and lemon juice together in a bowl until well combined. Season to taste. Set aside.

Arrange the figs on a serving platter. Roughly tear the mozzarella into shreds and scatter over the figs. Using the back of a wooden spoon, hold a pomegranate half in your hand, seeds facing down, and knock the peel until the seeds fall out over the figs. Repeat with other half.

Drizzle over the dressing, sprinkle with mint and serve.

chapter 03

Mount Carmel School Bush-Tucker Garden

Here come the Bunnies

I wake to the news that one of the world's most inspiring leaders and one of my personal heroes, Nelson Mandela, has died at the age of ninety-five. As I drive to Our Lady of Mount Carmel Catholic Primary School in inner-city Sydney, heavy with this sadness, I can't think of a more optimistic way to be spending the day. I will be surrounded by laughing children whose Indigenous heritage Mandela, through his lifelong fight against discrimination, would have revelled in.

While Mount Carmel's famous kitchen garden is the reason for my visit, today we're all a little distracted by football. The school is in Rabbitohs heartland, the legendary South Sydney Rugby League team owned by Hollywood superstar Russell Crowe. Two of its stars, Indigenous player Greg Inglis and New Zealander Jeff Lima, have just visited and there is an excited buzz in the playground. Rabbitohs players are the 'golden sons' of this disadvantaged suburb, and the students in their bright red uniforms and sun caps are zipping around swapping stories and showing off autographs. Greg Inglis is one of the greatest rugby league players of their generation. They'll remember this day for the rest of their lives – and as a passionate Bunnies supporter, so will I.

Two players from the South Sydney club come to the school every Friday and spend a few hours with the kindergarten class, listening to them read from their favourite books. Their visits are part of the 'Souths Cares' program, which encourages Indigenous students to go on to higher education. Greg Inglis understands the challenges better than most. He didn't finish high school and has recently returned to study, enrolling in a business course at The University of Sydney. In between footy training you'll find him sitting in the lecture theatres of the prestigious institution learning about accounting, financial planning and business law. He's the first person in his family to go to university. His message to the children is simple: it's never too late to discover the joys of learning.

As I negotiate the uneven concrete steps and playground tarmac cracking from tree roots, I can't help but wonder what difference it might have made if Greg Inglis' primary school had had a kitchen garden.

Food for thought

Our Lady of Mount Carmel Primary School sits high on a rocky outcrop in gritty Waterloo, surrounded by a small public park. Somehow on this tiny sandstone protrusion the school manages to squeeze in 130 students from kindergarten to Year 6. Almost three-quarters of them are Indigenous and many come from nearby housing estates. The educational odds against them are stark. Only 49 per cent of Aboriginal and Torres Strait Islander students complete their final years of schooling. This compares with 81 per cent in 2011 for non-Indigenous students.

While retention rates are improving incrementally, Mount Carmel knows that establishing a good foundation for a positive learning environment falls largely with them, at primary school. Instilling self-esteem and confidence in children is essential to opening them up to the joys of learning. Most of the students speak a language other than English at home. Developing relationships with their parents, who have often had a bad school experience themselves, is vital.

Principal John Farrell believes the rich cultural diversity of his school can be a source of great pride and harmony if channelled in the right direction. With this in mind Mount Carmel established its 'Leadership for Reconciliation' program. Children would be introduced to the richness of Indigenous language and traditions, including learning about Indigenous foods or 'bush tucker'. Encouraging students to grow and eat native foods would strengthen their cultural awareness and improve their understanding of where food comes from. And, as we all know, when learning can be tactile and hands-on it's bound to be more enjoyable.

But where could these inner-city Indigenous kids see their native foods being grown?

Few of the families had gardens. Most had lost their connection to Indigenous food traditions. Food without a barcode was rare in some households. Takeaways and frozen pizza were the more usual dinner-table offerings; fresh food and home-cooked meals were the exception. In fact, poor student nutrition generally had become an ongoing issue at the school. Teachers were increasingly finding that many students were coming to school hungry without having had a proper breakfast. This was not only affecting their health but their ability to concentrate and learn in class.

This led, in 2012, to one motivated parent initiating a scheme called 'Brekkie on the Mount' on Monday and Friday mornings. The program is sponsored by the Red Cross and run by the local Police Citizens Youth Club (PCYC) and community volunteers. For breakfast, students are served cereal, fruit and wholemeal toast. Not only has the program improved student nutrition but it has also boosted school attendance and punctuality on those days.

However, while the program was addressing the immediate food needs of the students, the school found they still lacked a deeper understanding about eating healthily. The program highlighted how disconnected from their food students – and some of their parents – had become.

The unfair but oft-quoted saying goes that 'Those who can "do" and those that can't "teach"'. Well, the teachers of Mount Carmel were going to prove that adage wrong. With no budget, little expertise and a whole lot of heart they were going to bring bush tucker to their students.

Plans were set in motion to expand an existing vegetable garden within the school's tiny grounds. It was to be an ambitious project that would transform the school community and show students, parents and teachers alike the true power of reconciliation.

Bringing the bush to the city

Established in 1858, Mount Carmel is one of Sydney's oldest Catholic schools. The spiritual guidance students receive is as important as their academic instruction. The school prayer, which is recited everyday, challenges students to 'be proud of who they are' and to give them the strength to 'give and forgive' (a prayer we could all benefit from reciting, no doubt). A bit of praying would be required to make a school bush-tucker garden a reality.

It all began serendipitously with a call late in 2010 from a local gardening organisation called Slow Grow. It had a grant of $5000 to start a vegetable garden and had identified Mount Carmel school as the beneficiary. Peter Farrell couldn't believe his good fortune. He gave the go-ahead for Slow Grow to begin transforming a corner of lawn above the school car park. Slow Grow built four raised garden beds and a small fruit orchard of citrus and peaches. They hired a landscaper who maintained the beds and began teaching students about composting.

In its early stages the garden was also used as a 'safe area' for children with behavioural difficulties. Through this 'Wingara' program they could do some gardening under the supervision of teacher Maree Ancich. The students could also bring a friend to help them water, weed and plant seeds such as corn and sunflowers.

In 2011 bush-food specialist Clarence Slockee from Sydney's Royal Botanic Gardens arrived with the TV crew from ABC's *Gardening Australia*. With the children, Clarence planted garden staples such as herbs and lettuce. He was also keen to showcase the students' Indigenous food heritage, so he helped them build a boomerang-shaped garden bed and began plotting out the plantings.

In went a native grevillea bush to attract birds with its nectar and flowers. The birds would act as natural pest controllers, eating insects from the garden. Next they planted native mint, then midgen (or midyim) berries, which are small and white with black spots and a sweet taste. A large hole was dug for a pepper tree, which has leaves with a pungent peppery aroma. Then in went a rainforest edible, the Davidson (or rainforest) plum, which has black plums with blood-red flesh. Davidson plums are packed with vitamin C and can be eaten straight off the bush or made into a jam. And finally a macadamia nut tree took pride of place in the centre of this native oasis. All the beds were mulched and watered-in well to protect the plants from the sun.

All gardens, though, need to be maintained. When teacher Alisha Bourke (right) arrived at Mount Carmel in 2012, the bush-tucker garden still wasn't being utilised to its potential. Alisha didn't know much about gardening but she knew if a maintenance program wasn't put in place the garden would soon be dead and all its educational benefits would be lost forever.

The school couldn't spare any time from the curriculum for the garden to be officially incorporated into her teaching duties, so Alisha decided to run a gardening club in her lunch hour. She resolved Thursday lunchtime would be Garden Club time. All Alisha had to do now was to convince some of the kids to give up part of their lunch break and get their hands dirty. It would be like herding cats.

How does your garden grow?

It's going to be a warm one. The sun is already burning through the light cloud cover and I can feel my clothes sticky against my skin. The children are coming down the playground steps from school assembly as photographer Alan Benson and I begin setting up our equipment. Kids in the Garden Club are running around in all directions, throwing school bags and doing cartwheels. They can barely contain their delight. They're putting on an afternoon tea in the school garden featuring their produce and their baking. And someone is going to take photographs of them that will be published in a book.

One student comes up to me and says, 'I've never met anyone who's written a book before. What's it like?' It's a very moving moment. 'It's great fun,' I eventually manage to say. 'You'll find out when you write one someday.' That puts a big smile on his face and he runs off to share our conversation with his friends.

Alisha Bourke is the personification of enthusiasm. With her bright cornflower-blue eyes, wavy blonde hair and raspy laugh, she could be mistaken for a high school student rather than a teacher. She still has a childlike wonder for life and a drive to deliver kids the best education she can. Teaching is clearly her calling.

Somehow she manages to organise this excited rabble into a workforce. The students are soon busy in the garden, harvesting produce for our afternoon tea. Long, rubbery fronds of glossy silverbeet are selected for tarts, lemons are picked for a tangy refreshing lemonade and ruby stalks of rhubarb are gathered for muffins. The garden is a free supermarket of tasty delights. Students pose with a basket overflowing with the squeaky fresh produce, clearly very proud they have grown all this themselves.

One of the keenest students is whippet-smart twelve-year-old Lauren Jones. With her curious, inquiring mind, I don't think she's going to have any trouble settling into her new high school next year. 'It will be sad to leave the garden,' she says. 'I'll miss it.'

Lauren has lived in Redfern all her life and started at Mount Carmel when she was six. The garden has been as much a part of her school life as her friends have. 'I just love doing things with my hands,' says Lauren. 'I didn't know anything about gardens when I first joined the Garden Club but I loved to see seeds grow and then the fruit and vegetables come up. It's so much fun.'

Lauren thinks she may do something to do with gardens or food when she leaves school. 'But that feels like such a long time to wait,' she says exasperatedly. This is a kid in a hurry. 'Everyone needs to eat food so if you know something about it you will always be able to get a job,' she observes astutely. A head on her shoulders beyond her years.

The Garden Club

At first, Alisha found it was easier to enlist younger children into the Garden Club. The Year 1s loved the idea of getting wet and kicking around in the mud. (It's my favourite part of gardening as well.) The older kids, however, were a little more reluctant to volunteer; lunch break was a time to hang out with their friends, not to 'study'. Incorporating cooking workshops into the gardening classes proved the perfect enticement. Even the Year 5s and 6s were tempted by the homemade rhubarb muffins and lemonade the class could enjoy at the end of a session. Garden Club numbers soon swelled to fifty students.

With her enthusiasm levels high, Alisha's gardening knowledge was growing but still limited. The garden's direction largely came from a community volunteer, Mary Bray, who had worked at the Royal Botanic Gardens and had run her own gardening business. Mary began transforming the garden using permaculture principals – companion planting, crop rotation, composting, mulching and using natural organic fertilisers and pest control methods. Alisha divided her students into several groups of mixed ages. They were responsible for weeding, hand-watering, propagating seeds, turning the compost, managing the worm farm, removing caterpillars and bugs, and harvesting the produce.

Most of the kids lived in apartments or in semi-detached cottages with little or no garden. This was often their first experience of growing anything – particularly things that they could eat. 'One of my students, Liam, was never really interested in the gardening. He would often get bored or distracted,' Alisha tells me. 'But the day he saw us picking a butternut pumpkin and making it into a pumpkin soup he just got hooked. He could see the reason we were working so hard in the garden. He could see the end result.' A seed that was planted in the ground and looked after with a little water became a pumpkin that was then transformed into a delicious, nutritious soup. Why do you need to explain miracles to children when you can give them a garden?

The garden crops have become more ambitious over time. In the first year the club planted passionfruit bushes, tomatoes and lots of herbs, then sugar snaps and snow peas, radish, lettuce and silverbeet. In the second year, beds were filled with potatoes, eggplants, more tomatoes and herbs, cucumbers, spinach, swedes, Asian greens, broad beans and artichokes. They have also put in what has been a successful and very popular raspberry bush and strawberry patch.

Having many hands makes light work where organic pest control is concerned. Patrols of tiny fingers are sent into the fruit trees to pick off aphids. Less popular but very effective is hand-picking caterpillars from the kale and broccoli and then giving them a gentle 'squish'. Sprays made from soaked tomato leaves are another way of controlling aphids, thrips, spider mites and other pests.

The garden has sandy soil that doesn't hold much water and endures a very hot afternoon sun so keeping watering up is always the challenge. Mary has incorporated manure and compost into the beds and helped the soil retain moisture by top-coating it with a lucerne mulch. There are plans to install a rainwater tank when funds become available.

The water-hardy crops such as the silverbeet, herbs and Asian greens tend to thrive the most but Alisha says most of the fruit and vegetables have been remarkably successful. 'The kids' favourites are probably the strawberries,' she says. 'They're sweet and fast-growing, and finding a ripe berry under the dense leaf cover before the caterpillars get to it is like a treasure hunt!' Mildew devastated the pumpkin crop but the students still managed to salvage a 2-kilogram specimen – which became the pumpkin soup Liam still talks about.

Kids in the kitchen

The cooking classes in the school teaching kitchen are a highlight for the students. Alisha and fellow teacher Helen Thornborough (opposite), a wonderful home cook, organise them into groups, each responsible for one dish. Helen has donated many of the kitchen utensils herself, so under-resourced is the school's cooking programme. Of course the kids don't notice that their implements are second-hand. The kitchen is abuzz with activity as each group begins preparing the ingredients. Rarely have I seen such focus and concentration with children this age. They are engrossed.

Alisha has found that many of her students come with very little food knowledge. Their experience of cooking at home has largely been reheating a frozen meal in the microwave. 'Some days the only fresh fruit or vegetable some students eat comes from our kitchen garden,' she says. 'Many of my kids didn't know that potatoes grew in the ground, for instance, or how eggplants, corn or pumpkins grew.' Watching the students expertly slice, dice and chop in the school's kitchen, it is difficult to picture the rudimentary skills they initially possessed.

The recipes Helen selects are simple to make and nutritious, but most importantly they have to pass the 'taste test'. During these classes students get to see how easily fresh produce can be transformed into meals. The misconception that cooking is difficult is something many of their parents believe as well. 'One of the dishes the kids love is pesto noodles, which is just pesto sauce tossed through warm spaghetti,' Helen says, as she shows one student how to fold the flour through the rhubarb muffin batter. 'Spaghetti can be slurped and sucked up so it's lots of fun to eat and the fresh garden basil in the pesto

is simple but delicious.' Other favourites include stir-fried Asian greens, broad bean and feta bruschetta, babaghanoush, broccoli soup, herb and cream cheese snails, squash bake and spinach rice. I notice that most of these recipes contain vegetables kids would normally turn their noses up at. 'Yes, I know!' agrees Helen. 'But when they grow these vegetables themselves, they can't wait to taste them.'

A trellis table in the garden is soon spread with our afternoon tea. Students are eager for the photos to be taken so they can scoff down the tarts and then dart into the plates of muffins, lemonade spilling down their faces. They're sitting in their garden, eating food they've prepared themselves using produce they've grown with their own hands. I have witnessed few more inspiring occasions.

Changing food habits

It's not just the students who have developed a newfound appreciation for fresh food through the Garden Club – their parents get the gardening bug as well. Alisha says one dad, who previously could never be coaxed through the school gates, comes into the garden especially for the radishes. 'He just loves them,' Alisha beams proudly. (The 'stick and carrot' metaphor may have to be replaced with 'stick and radish'.) One Garden Club student even pestered her mother to start a home veggie patch and her family is now growing some herbs and greens in pots on their balcony.

The students are becoming more familiar with a wider range of vegetables and influencing the produce their family buys during the weekly supermarket shop.

'One parent told me that her daughter wanted to put an eggplant in the shopping trolley,' remembers Alisha. 'When her mother responded that she didn't think she liked eggplants, her daughter said, "I do now. We grow and cook them at school." Her mother was quite taken aback.' When the mother shared this story, Alisha gave her a recipe for diced eggplant fried simply on a sandwich press, and now the whole family enjoys the dish.

Growing our future

Being able to eat what they grow has become a great motivator for the Mount Carmel students. In fact Alisha now gets stopped by the kindies who say they can't wait to join Garden Club when they are older. In 2013 the garden was incorporated into Alisha's official teaching duties and she now often conducts her science lessons there. She finds that growing and gardening makes biology and chemistry so much more accessible. The students do experiments using seeds and sprouts, and learn about insects and birds while getting a 'field experience' at the same time. 'Taking them out of a bricks and mortar classroom just seems to make their learning experience more enjoyable and stimulating. They forget they're at school and not meant to be enjoying themselves,' she laughs.

The garden has become the kids' classroom. The knowledge and skills they're developing here can't be taught in a four-walled, fluoro-lit, air-conditioned room. They're interacting with the real world, the natural world, a world where they can see the cycles of life and death and renewal play out in front of their eyes. These kids are becoming resilient, thoughtful and self-aware. *They* think they're just having fun. What they're actually doing is learning about co-operation in a competitive world. They're learning about conservation in a world where consumerism is king. They're learning that their Indigenous ancestors knew this all along.

I hope as they make their way into the world beyond the school gates they will keep what they have learnt here in this garden close to their hearts. If they can, our future will be in good hands.

LEMON MYRTLE

When to plant?
Hot humid climate: Year-round
Hot dry climate: Not suitable
Cool temperate climate: September–March

What to grow? Small potted shrub will grow up to 6 metres.

Where to grow? Sub-tropical but will tolerate cooler climates.

I like . . . slightly acidic soil.

I don't like . . . water-logged soils.

Feed me . . . plant me in enriched composted soil.

Give me a drink . . . keep me moist.

DAVIDSON PLUM

When to plant?
Hot humid climate: Year-round
Hot dry climate: Not suitable
Cool temperate climate: November–March

What to grow? From seed or seedling. Grows to about 6–8 metres.

Where to grow? In a sheltered, part-shaded part of the garden.

I like . . . warm weather.

I don't like . . . damaging winds.

Feed me . . . with a high-phosphorous fertiliser.

Give me a drink . . . keep me well-watered.

MOUNTAIN PEPPER

When to plant?
Hot humid climate: Not suitable
Hot dry climate: Not suitable
Cool temperate climate: Year-round

What to grow? Both male and female seedlings if you want berries.

Where to grow? Climates with good rainfall, cold winters and mild summers.

I like . . . to be planted in soil with well-rotted compost and manure.

I don't like . . . heat.

Feed me . . . sprinkle Dynamic Lifter around my base in early winter.

Give me a drink . . . I like moist soil.

STRAWBERRIES

When to plant?
Hot humid climate: Year-round
Hot dry climate: June–July
Cool temperate climate: Year-round

What to grow? Buy certified disease-free plants from nurseries.

Where to grow? Plant seedlings with crown of plant just covered.

I like . . . well-drained soil with plenty of humus.

I don't like . . . frosts and pests such as slugs and birds. Mulch with pine needles or black plastic to prevent mould.

Feed me . . . a liquid fertiliser during the growing season.

Give me a drink . . . regularly.

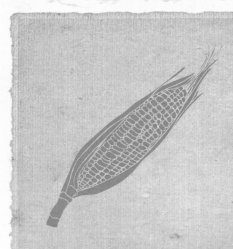

CORN

When to plant?
Hot humid climate: Year-round
Hot dry climate: September–January
Cool temperate climate: September–January

What to grow? Seed is best sown directly in well-manured soil, but it can also be raised in pots or tubes in a warm spot and planted after germination.

Where to grow? Plant corn seed in blocks of three or more rows, rather than long single rows. This allows for a more even dispersal of pollen, producing cobs with even and consistent kernel production. Establish 30 or more plants per sowing.

I like . . . warm to hot conditions.

I don't like . . . strong winds.

Feed me . . . liquid feed once a week with a mix of diluted kelp and fish emulsion at half strength.

Give me a drink . . . water soil well and don't water again until seeds germinate or they will rot.

MELONS

When to plant?
Hot humid climate: December–March
Hot dry climate: April–July
Cool temperate climate: October–December

What to grow? Plant seed in trays and plant out in 4–6 weeks. Best planted when soil temperatures are between 21°C and 35°C.

Where to grow? In a large bed, or compact varieties can be grown in pots with good compost.

I like . . . a long warm season to mature.

I don't like . . . direct contact with soil. Mulch with straw.

Feed me . . . side dress with compost or manure tea every 2–3 weeks.

Give me a drink . . . I like regular deep watering but not overhead or mildew will form.

Melon salad

Serves 6 as a side

I love using fruit in my salads. The addition of freshly cracked pepper in this recipe gives the melon a savoury note. This salad goes well with barbecued steak or prawns.

½ watermelon, skin removed

½ rockmelon, skin and seeds removed

½ honeydew melon, skin and seeds removed

¼ cup (60 ml) lime juice

1 tablespoon honey

small handful mint leaves, thinly sliced

salt and freshly ground black pepper

Chop the melons into 2 cm cubes and place in a serving bowl. Mix the lime juice and honey together and drizzle over the top. Season with salt and pepper, and sprinkle over the mint. Toss gently.

Serve immediately.

Lemon myrtle vinaigrette

Makes about ⅓ cup (80 ml)

Lemon myrtle has a bright, citrussy flavour like that of lemons, limes and lemongrass. It complements many culinary delights, from fish and chicken to ice-cream and sorbet. I get my stock of lemon myrtle powder and Tasmanian mountain pepper from A Taste of the Bush: atasteofthebush.com.au. Check their website for your nearest supplier.

½ teaspoon lemon myrtle powder

¼ cup (60 ml) macadamia oil

1 tablespoon white wine vinegar

1 tablespoon lemon juice

¼ teaspoon sugar

1 teaspoon Tasmanian mountain pepper

pinch of salt

Place the lemon myrtle powder, macadamia oil, vinegar and lemon juice in a bowl and whisk well. Add the sugar, mountain pepper and salt, and stir to combine.

This vinaigrette will keep for a week in a sealed jar in the fridge.

Bolognaise sauce with tagliatelle

Serves 8

'Spag bol' always tops surveys of Australians' favourite dish to cook at home. It seems everyone has their own recipe for this Italian classic. Mine was handed down to me by my Italian nonna. Just kidding. My heritage is actually Indian– South African, but this bolognaise recipe was given to me by the chef/owner of a *pensione* I stayed at in Orvieto near Rome. I've been cooking it almost once a month, at least, since.

1 tablespoon olive oil

50 g smoked speck or pancetta, sliced into matchsticks

2 large onions, diced

2 large carrots, diced

2 stalks celery, diced

4 cloves garlic, finely chopped

2 sprigs thyme

1 sprig rosemary

1 fresh bay leaf

2 anchovy fillets

500 g organic beef mince

500 g organic pork and veal mince

1 cup (500 ml) red wine

3 × 400 g tins chopped tomatoes

2 tablespoons tomato paste (puree)

salt and freshly ground black pepper

handful chopped flat-leaf parsley

tagliatelle, to serve

grated parmesan, to serve

Heat the olive oil in a heavy-based casserole over medium heat. Add the speck or pancetta and fry for 6 minutes or until it is crisp, just beginning to brown and releases most of its fat. Add the onion, carrot and celery, cover with the lid and cook over medium–low heat for 15 minutes or until soft.

Add the garlic, thyme, rosemary, bay leaf and anchovy fillets and fry for 1 minute. Turn up the heat, add the beef and pork mince and fry, stirring until well browned. Add the red wine and cook until it has almost evaporated. Add the chopped tomato and bring to a boil. Turn the heat down to low and simmer for 3 hours, stirring occasionally.

Ten minutes before the sauce is cooked, add the tomato paste, season with salt and pepper and stir through the parsley.

Meanwhile, cook the tagliatelle in plenty of salted boiling water until al dente, then drain.

Serve the bolognaise sauce with the tagliatelle, sprinkled with grated parmesan.

Roasted wild mushroom pizzettes

Serves 8

This is a great recipe to cook with the kids. Help them make the dough and use the oven – they can pile on the toppings themselves.

olive oil, to drizzle

green leaf salad, to serve

DOUGH

600 g plain flour, plus extra for dusting

pinch of salt

1 × 7 g sachet yeast

½ teaspoon sugar

1¾ cups (430 ml) lukewarm water

1 tablespoon olive oil

TOPPING

1 cup (250 ml) tomato passata

200 g mixed wild mushrooms, cleaned and sliced

110 g buffalo mozzarella, torn

½ cup (40 g) finely grated parmesan

2 tablespoons thyme leaves, plus extra sprigs to garnish

salt and freshly ground black pepper

To make the dough, sift the flour and salt into a bowl and stir in the yeast and sugar. Combine the water and olive oil in a jug, then pour into the dry ingredients and mix with a flat-bladed knife until the mixture comes together. Tip out onto a floured work surface and knead for 10 minutes or until smooth and elastic. Place the dough in an oiled bowl and cover with plastic film and a tea towel. Set aside in a warm place for 30 minutes or until doubled in size.

Preheat the oven to 250°C. Lightly oil two large baking trays and place in the oven to warm.

When the dough has risen, knock out the air with your fist and divide into eight. Roll out each portion into a disc. Spread over some tomato passata and top with the mushrooms, mozzarella, parmesan and thyme, then season with salt and pepper.

Bake for 15–20 minutes or until the cheese has melted and the crust sounds hollow when tapped.

Drizzle with olive oil and garnish with thyme. Serve immediately with a green leaf salad.

Corn cobs with herb butter

Serves 4

Corn seems to be one of the first vegetables kids adore. It's tasty and packed with fibre, nutrients and carbohydrates. And smearing on a little butter won't hurt win the little ones over, either.

4 corn cobs in husks
60 g butter, softened
1 teaspoon grated horseradish
2 tablespoons chopped mixed herbs (parsley, oregano, basil, etc)
salt and freshly ground black pepper

Place the corn on a microwave plate and cook on high heat for 10 minutes or until the corn kernels are soft. Leave to cool for a few minutes. Alternatively, bring 2 litres of salted water to the boil in a large saucepan, add the corn and boil for 15 minutes or until soft. Remove and drain on paper towel.

In a small bowl, mix together the butter, horseradish, herbs, and salt and pepper to taste. Slather the herb butter over the cobs, re-wrapping the husks over the cob.

Place the cooked cobs in their husks on a preheated barbecue for 2 minutes for a final char and smoky flavour, before serving.

Lemonade

Makes about 1 litre

This lemonade recipe has been generously shared by the Our Lady of Mount Carmel primary school. Its simplicity belies its deliciousness.

1¼ cups (275 g) caster sugar
2 cups (500 ml) boiling water
1 cup (250 ml) freshly squeezed lemon juice
1 cup (250 ml) cold water
lemon slices, mint leaves and ice-cubes, to serve

Place the sugar in a large heatproof bowl or jug. Add the boiling water and stir to dissolve. Add the lemon juice and cold water and stir. Refrigerate until cool.

Serve in tall glasses with lemon slices, mint and ice-cubes.

Rhubarb muffins

Makes 12

The kids (and adults) in your family are going to love these moist and moreish muffins. This is also a recipe from Mount Carmel school, which I've adapted and tweaked by adding some rhubarb pieces on top of each muffin.

½ cup (140 g) vanilla yoghurt

2 tablespoons unsalted butter, melted

2 tablespoons vegetable oil

1 egg

1⅓ cups (200 g) plain flour

¾ cup (165 g) brown sugar

½ teaspoon bicarbonate of soda

½ teaspoon salt

3 stems rhubarb, trimmed and finely diced

TOPPING

¼ cup (55 g) brown sugar

½ teaspoon ground cinnamon

½ teaspoon ground nutmeg

¼ cup (30 g) ground almonds

2 teaspoons unsalted butter, melted

2 stems rhubarb, trimmed and cut into 12 × 3 cm pieces

Preheat the oven to 180°C fan-forced (200°C conventional). Grease 12 paper muffin cases and place them in 12-hole muffin tray.

In a bowl, stir together the yoghurt, melted butter, oil and egg.

In a separate large bowl, stir together the flour, sugar, bicarbonate of soda and salt. Pour the wet ingredients into the dry ones and stir just to combine; don't over-mix. Gently fold in the diced rhubarb.

Spoon the batter into the prepared muffin cases until two-thirds full.

For the topping, rub together the sugar, cinnamon, nutmeg, ground almonds and melted butter. Spoon over the muffins and top with a piece of rhubarb.

Bake for 25 minutes or until the tops spring back when lightly pressed. Allow to cool in the tray before serving.

Cherry choc chip ice-cream sandwiches

Makes 18

These are the heavenly ice-cream sandwiches of your childhood.
Even better – the ice-cream recipe doesn't begin with a custard,
and so avoids the 'will it or won't it?' curdling fear.

2 cups (500 ml) thickened cream
1 cup (250 ml) full-cream milk
¾ cup (165 g) caster sugar, plus 1 teaspoon extra
1½ cups (225 g) frozen cherries, partially thawed
85 g dark chocolate (70 per cent cocoa), roughly chopped
36 plain chocolate biscuits (Arnott's Choc Ripple biscuits or similar)

In a large bowl, whisk together the cream, milk and sugar, and stir until the sugar dissolves. Churn in an ice-cream machine according to the manufacturer's instructions.

Toss the cherries with the extra teaspoon of sugar. Add the cherries, along with any juice, and the chocolate to the ice-cream mixture. Transfer to a container with a lid and freeze until firm enough to scoop.

To assemble the sandwiches, spread ⅓ cup (80 g) of ice-cream over a biscuit and top with another biscuit. Repeat with the remaining biscuits and ice-cream. Wrap tightly in baking paper and freeze until ready to serve. The sandwiches will keep for 24 hours in the freezer.

Turramurra Lookout Community Garden

Road rescue

I've been sitting in this traffic snarl on the Pacific Highway on Sydney's North Shore for almost an hour now – and I'm still 5 kilometres away from the Turramurra Lookout Community Garden. Turramurra, which means 'big hill', has some of the worst gridlock in Sydney. Its original Indigenous inhabitants, the Guringai people, would struggle to recognise it now. Although it sits bordered by national parks boasting some of the best examples of blue gum and turpentine high forest, all I can see are bumper-to-bumper cars, apartment developments and suburban crush. Along this high ridge, 'leafy' Turramurra isn't so leafy any more. I see my turn-off up ahead and pull out to find a park, relieved I've finally escaped the interminable crawl. Then I am reminded of something I read recently: 'You are the traffic you complain about.'

I virtually stumble into the garden before I realise it. There are no fences or gates or locks. The garden stretches right up to the highway, with trimmed lavender and rosemary bushes and herb patches spilling out over the narrow footpath. The extensive herb hedges act

Here is a lush thriving allotment just metres from the choking highway traffic.

as a 'swale', absorbing water runoff from the road and reducing soil erosion in the garden. They also act as a pollution and sound buffer. I'm surprised how little traffic noise I can hear, even though the busy highway is just 10 metres away.

The tiered garden follows the contours of the hillside and falls sharply towards a dense copse of rainforest. The 3000 square metre area is divided into a few dozen allotments, each personalised with handmade signs, wooden posts and repurposed fencing materials. The adornments give the garden a sense of fun and playfulness. I smile as I notice a lovingly made scarecrow standing guard.

I feel a light drizzle on my face and look up to see grey clouds overhead, gathering with urgency. No one else seems to notice. The garden is peppered with people in bright raincoats, parkas and gumboots busily weeding or planting new seedlings. It's as if they're suspended in a gentle meditation.

It's quite surreal. Here is a lush thriving allotment dense with vegetable patches just metres down the slope from choking highway traffic. Two such contrasting uses of land side by side. Humans never cease to amaze.

Urban farming

Over the past century there has been a huge change in the way Australians grow their food. A hundred years ago almost every family in every house on every quarter acre block had its own veggie patch. Not any more.

After the Second World War suburban backyards ceased to be major sites for food production. New convenience foods such as *The Jetsons*-style 'frozen meals' or powdered cake mixes enticed us out of our gardens and into the supermarkets. You had better things to do with your time than garden, the advertisers told us. There was now an activity called 'leisure' where housewives were encouraged to become 'consumers' and leave the dreary job of growing food and meal preparation to food corporations.

But we didn't foresee the wider consequences that abandoning our farming roots would have. Over the decades, as we filled our shopping trolleys with more and more processed food, we also lost an appreciation for where it had come from, who had grown it for us, how it was grown and what went into it. This disconnect has led to many of the malaises we see on the television news each night – food contamination scares, obesity epidemics, cancers, environmental damage, climate change and social isolation.

We're slowly discovering that food gardening did more than just provide us with nourishing home-grown produce. Growing our own food kept us rooted in nature. When our hands worked the soil, it reminded us that we are not separate from nature but in fact *part* of nature. We understood the cycles of the planet. We noticed the seasons changing, the weather and the climate. Removing ourselves from this intimate relationship left us empty and depleted. Buying more consumer gadgets (yes, even the latest iPhone) didn't fill this aching void. We didn't realise we missed the hidden physiological and emotional benefits that simply watching things grow had provided us with.

Reconnecting with these lost roots isn't easy. We've literally run out of space to garden. Our cities have encroached on our market gardens and fertile lands. The urban sprawl has become relentless, with our McMansions leading the charge. Australians now own some of the largest houses in the world. The average floor area of a new freestanding house in Australia is 243 square metres. According to the Australian Bureau of Statistics, the average new home built in Australia in 2011 was 10 per cent bigger than its counterpart in the United States and 9 per cent bigger than in New Zealand. These monolithic homes we've created are often fitted out with their own media rooms and spas. They are so enormous they often cannibalise the entire block of land right to the fence-line, squeezing out space for anything else. (Why go to all the trouble of looking after a garden when you can have a low-maintenance cinema-sized flat-screen television instead, burning up fossil fuels through electricity?)

For those of us who've downsized to inner-city apartments, the dearth of outdoor space is even more dire. My suburb of Potts Point in Sydney has one of the highest population densities of any urban area in the world, with 13 000 people per square kilometre. We literally live on top of one another in our vertical villages. And in these villages economics is god, not nature. When a square metre of real estate can cost as much as $26 000, gardens are almost always going to lose out to bedrooms and car spaces.

Gardening is reclaiming our cities, inch by inch, spade by spade.

But even with these barriers the desire to grow is strong. Gardening is reclaiming our cities gradually, inch by inch, spade by spade. We're leaving our homes and banding together to transform wasted parkland, forgotten alleyways, corridors, footpaths and fences into productive green spaces. Some call it no more than a passing fad. Others believe we could be witnessing an enduring cultural shift.

Community gardeners are staking their claim. In 2010 the Australian City Farms and Community Gardens Network had 212 community gardens and edible schoolyards listed on its register. These community gardens, single plots of land gardened collectively by a group of people, have sprouted throughout the country – in cities and suburbs, in regional towns, even along freeways.

According to the Australia Institute's 'Grow your own' study published in 2014, 13 per cent of respondents said they planned to begin a veggie patch in their home or in a community garden within the next twelve months. The study found South Australians, Tasmanians and Victorians were more likely to be growing food than households in other states. More surprisingly, 52 per cent of Australians in the study reported they were already growing some food. This equates to 4.7 million households.

When asked for their reasons for growing their own food, most interviewees cited the health and financial benefits, as well as the social interaction involved. Other factors included reducing food miles, improving local food security and helping convert wasted urban land into green spaces.The study also revealed some interesting facts about who is growing food. They are just as likely to be male or female, young or old, Labor or Liberal voters, first-generation migrants or not. The only demographic characteristic that clearly delineates food growers is that households with children are more likely to grow food. Interest in the grow-your-own-food movement tends to peak when there is a crisis, such as during the Second World War when 'Dig For Victory' was the mantra, or in the 1970s during the 'Peak Oil' crunch that sent food prices skywards. Current concerns about climate change and extreme weather events have certainly made some consumers more aware of the fragile link between the environment and our food supply.

It is experiencing a current wave of popularity, but community gardening has been around for many decades. Australia's first official community garden was established almost thirty years ago in Nunawading, Victoria, in 1977. The local council donated some vacant land and enthusiasts have maintained the garden ever since. Almost four decades later, these plots – the original collective acts of community – are still thriving on the outskirts of Melbourne. More importantly the gardeners' trailblazing achievements are stirring others to follow suit, like the gardeners at the Turramurra Lookout Community Garden.

Digging for victory

'Hello, Indira,' comes a voice emerging from the shed. I turn to see a man in his 60s, in a hat and khakis, with a wide welcoming grin on his face. 'I'm John Dailey. How about a cuppa?'

John (right) invites me into his shed. It is the cleanest, most organised 'man cave' I've ever seen. It's more like a granny flat with its own solar-panelled electricity providing hot water for tea and coffee, armchairs and a rug on the concrete floor, tools all neatly labelled and arranged along the galvanised steel walls and a bright harvest of pumpkins displayed on a shelf.

John Dailey is clearly proud of what his Turramurra community gardeners have managed to achieve in just a few short years. 'We're getting there,' he says in his – what I will begin to know well – typically understated manner. John is now retired but spent his career running recruitment firms and insurance agencies. He clearly knows how to manage and organise people, which are essential skills in any community venture.

Just four years ago, this land was a rarely used council park wedged between

a retirement village and a railway line. Its steep incline made it difficult to walk around in or undertake any real leisure activities. It was well known as a late-night gathering spot for young pot-smokers. In a suburb where similar-sized plots of land could sell for $1 million, ratepayers were clearly not getting value for money.

John and his wife, Sue, have been Turramurra residents for many years. Now retired, their long-held desire to grow their own food was restricted by the tall trees in their yard, which blocked most of the light. Several of John's friends had similar issues and the idea was soon planted – so to speak – to start Turramurra's first community garden.

In 2009 they began discussing possible garden locations with the Ku-ring-gai Council. However, they found unexpected opposition from some local residents. Some of Turramurra's well-heeled locals believed community gardens were 'untidy' and would attract 'the wrong sort of people'. John and his group recruited the help of a local councillor and town planner, Julie Antville, and were soon armed with considered responses to most concerns. Although at first the Council was sceptical, it could see many of the benefits a community garden would bring – a better managed public green space, activity for young and elderly residents, improved local access to fresh food, and a way of building a stronger sense of community.

The existing park at the Turramurra Lookout on a busy stretch of the Pacific Highway soon became a location frontrunner, although John initially thought its steep aspect and water erosion issues would make it a 'poisoned chalice' as a garden. Its biggest advantage was its neighbours – or more to the point, the lack of them. There was only the retirement village to consult with and it was more than happy that the park would be turned into a more user-friendly space for its residents.

> Just four years ago this land was a rarely used council park.

The Turramurra Lookout Park was morphing into the Turramurra Lookout Community Garden. The wrong sort of people were about to move in.

The wrong sort of people

The founding group behind the garden had an impressive combined resume: John with his project and people management skills, Julie Antville with her town planning expertise, the ex-deputy head of St Ives Primary School, Tina Howard, and Doug Williamson, who with his background in house-washing and landscaping brought invaluable technical and practical experience.

The first task was to draw up some architectural and engineering plans so the interim management committee could understand the scale of the building works required and, as importantly, the budget that would be needed. It was going to be costly, even with council backing, and it would help to have a benefactor. They needed to look no further

than across the road. Literally. The Turramurra branch of the Bendigo Bank had its offices on the corner of the Pacific Highway directly opposite the garden site. The bank enjoyed supporting community projects, although it had never sponsored a community garden before. The garden's management team were enthusiastic but inexperienced garden builders. The bank did what banks rarely do – it took a gamble. It agreed to donate $20 000 to the project.

John and his team were now spending hours every day putting plans in place for the initial landscaping, which required earthmoving equipment (and would swallow up half their budget). For days, trucks and diggers dug into the boggy clay soil, clearing and levelling, until the park resembled a dirt pit. There was no going back now.

After the roadside boon and swale were constructed, work began on building several dry stone walls that would create a series of terraced plots and help with water retention. Almost forty trailer-loads of council-donated sandstone blocks were moved in. With help from a TAFE stonemason, a series of beautifully crafted walls started to give the garden some shape. Several raised communal beds were slotted in at the entrance and twenty-five or so individual plots were marked out further down the hillside. They were filled with rich compost and organic material to improve the clay soils below.

A food forest took root at the bottom of the slope, with citrus and fig trees, native finger limes, tamarillos, nuts, apples and peaches. A native beehive of tiny stingless sugarbag bees (*Tetragonula carbonaria*) was settled near the fruit trees to help with garden pollination. I'm enamoured with them. (Their being stingless certainly deepens my bond.) Next to them went some worm farms and a composting system. And the council donated a 4000 litre-capacity rainwater tank that was installed against the shed to capture roof run-off and reduce the garden's mains water usage.

The Turramurra Lookout was beginning to look like a garden. All they needed now were some gardeners.

That's when good neighbours become good friends

As the garden took shape, there was a lot of interest from passers-by about the strange goings-on at the old park. As part of the sharing philosophy of the new garden, locals were openly encouraged to pick the footpath rosemary and hedge herbs. 'Who would put a vegetable garden on a highway?' they asked, and 'Didn't most people in Turramurra have their own backyards anyway?' But, as it turned out, John and his team were not alone. Dozens of residents had the community garden 'itch' as well. Many had retired, lost partners, downsized to apartments or had no suitable space to grow food. Garden membership soon filled up. It cost $50 a year to become a member and $50 a year to rent a plot. When the garden opened in June 2010, they already had 100 keen locals on board.

The demographic mix is interesting. Of the fifty members, forty or so are active gardeners. There are retirees, yes, but there are also people in their early 20s and families with young children. Fiona and her three daughters, Mia (pictured front-centre, page 146), Sophie (page 143) and Olivia (page 145), had never grown anything before and saw the garden as a way to learn about growing food while making some new friends. In their small plot, they are growing beans, rocket and strawberries. Watching the girls excitedly pick a ripe fig or fresh bean, you would think they had been *born* in a cabbage patch. Garden life is already second nature to them.

A woman in a broad-rimmed pink hat works in a plot nearby. Annie's Chinese background means she grew up in a family that always grew their own food. Her plot is bursting with Asian greens, herbs and climbing beans all expertly tied and trellised. She has suspended paper butterflies over her crops to keep away cabbage moth. She says it works as a natural pest control. I believe her.

Michael, one of the residents at the North Haven retirement village next door, has been looking after the fig trees, which are dense with plump fruit. 'They're selling for $3 at the supermarket so we've had a few pilfered. I do a patrol in the evenings,' he says, brandishing his walking stick, 'to make sure the buggers stay away.' I picture a fig thief finding Michael – a broad-shouldered ex-army officer – hiding in the bushes and smile. Under the gruff exterior Michael is an old softy. He delights in being surrounded by the children and generously shares his gardening knowledge with them. 'Life in a retirement village can be very dull,' he says. 'The garden has given me a new hobby – something to look forward to. And the spread at the Saturday morning teas is worth the membership fees alone!' I soon see what he means. There are some good bakers in the gardening club. Tables have been covered with a picnic feast – chocolate cake, orange poppy-seed muffins, apple tea cake, coconut slice, chicken sandwiches and fresh figs from the garden. Morning tea during the Saturday 'working bee' has become a tradition, sign-posting to all gardeners that they can leave their communal duties and begin work on their own plots.

The harmony among this group is obvious. They genuinely enjoy each other's company. They've defied the inevitable isolation that city life can bring and become friends. What else but a garden would bring such a disparate group of people together?

Garden goodness

General jobs in the Turramurra garden are managed with a roster system. Most gardeners take turns to dig over the compost heaps and collect worm juice and castings from the

worm farms. The bees look after themselves. Then there is weeding and pruning, mulching the paths to keep weeds at bay or preparing a bed with a green manure crop so it can be left fallow for a season to replenish its nutrients. There is always something to do in a garden.

The garden loosely follows permaculture and organic principles – no harmful pesticides or chemicals are used, companion planting is promoted to encourage natural resistance, and vegetables, herbs and flowers are planted to attract good bugs and pollinators. A wide variety of staples are grown, from tomatoes to lettuces, but there are always some unusual finds such as a heritage breed eggplant or purple broccoli. There is a lot of seed sharing between growers of successful crops.

As much effort is put into keeping bugs away as growing food. 'Why put in all the hard work if the bugs are the only ones who enjoy it?' says Sue Dailey, very sensibly. White butterfly is a regular torment and Sue has found the best way to protect crops is with netting and frames. This also helps with keeping out the bandicoots and rabbits. Bottles with a little fruit juice at the bottom have proven a good way of trapping fruit fly and some gardeners use a molasses spray, which discourages egg-laying.

Most of the pathways have been hedged with good insect attractant flowers such as calendula, nasturtium, Queen Anne's lace, red clover and fennel. The garden sources its 'good bug' seed mix from Green Harvest or Greenpatch seeds. Most vegetables have done well in the plots, particularly pumpkins, cucumbers, squash, snake beans, spinach, silverbeet, beetroot and cabbages. Sue says there is always a glut of zucchini and more chillies and peppers than everyone can consume. What hasn't done well are some of the root vegetables such as carrots and parsnips, possibly because the soil is too clayey and can get waterlogged.

And while the garden hasn't been as productive as they had hoped – plans for a weekly produce stall have been put on hold until turnover can be boosted – everything they grow certainly tastes better. 'I've never eaten such delicious tomatoes as the ones we grow here,' says John.

When I visit, everyone is especially busy, with seeds being collected, planted and labelled for the annual fundraising plant sale in a few weeks' time. I spy some purple kale

seedlings and sprouting broccoli that will do very well on my balcony. Once you've got the bug, you just can't stop coveting a new edible to try out. The sale is not only a chance to raise much-needed funds to keep the garden running but also provides an opportunity to introduce more local residents to the joys of community gardening. A glasshouse has just been built near the entrance driveway (using a set of complicated instructions that would have put IKEA to shame). Everyone hopes the louvered-walled hothouse is going to help triple the number of seedlings they can germinate and sell this year.

Veggie vandalism

Managing a diverse group of community gardeners isn't easy. There are strong personalities from different backgrounds with different motivations. The challenge is to find the commonalities and build on those. John and the management team had spent considerable time studying community garden models from around the world. As an insurance specialist, John wanted the garden to remain under Ku-ring-gai Council's control and not be incorporated into a separate business, so any insurance issues would fall under the Council's responsibility. New gardeners are also asked to sign a set of garden guidelines before they join so they understand their responsibilities to the garden and each other. A management team of seven is elected each year and they meet six times a year to discuss any issues and plan strategies.

The model usually works well. Any grumblings are soon nipped in the bud. If someone thinks someone else's crops are blocking the light in their garden, solutions and compromises are reached. If someone else wants to move their plot to a better location, everything is done within reason to make this possible.

But despite the best of intentions, some conflicts arose that couldn't be resolved and a few people left the garden unhappy with their experience. It was one of these disillusioned souls that police believe may have been responsible for an overnight vandalism attack in the garden in March 2014 just before the annual seedling sale.

Gardeners arrived that Saturday morning to find their allotments had been ransacked. Pots and seedlings in the greenhouse had been upended, the beehive had been kicked over, the watering system had been cut and the pond pump destroyed along with all the native frogs and fish. It was devastating. There was at least $2000 worth of damage. Worse still, most of the seedlings for the garden sale had been destroyed.

Police and a forensics team were soon on the scene and from the targeted damage believed it was a wilful attack by someone who knew the garden well. News stories ran in the local papers but the culprit was never apprehended. The garden community rallied together and doubled their efforts for the plant sale, with some members baking extra cakes to make up for the seedling losses, and they still managed to raise $300.

After the vandalism there was talk of fencing in the garden, even though that went against its open welcome philosophy. In the end the Council agreed instead to consider installing better lighting and possibly mounting a CCTV camera. 'There's a good strong spirit in the garden and it will take more than this attack to dampen our commitment,' says John. I'm impressed by their resilience and determination not to be disheartened by this unsettling incident. I, on the other hand, still feel quite angry at the selfishness and cruelty of the assault.

Smell the roses

Resilient communities always manage to bounce back from setbacks. The Turramurra Lookout Community Gardeners have taken the shocking vandalism attack in their gum-booted stride.

'The garden has become a shining light for the Ku-ring-gai Council,' John says. 'We've shown that community gardens can work in Turramurra and bring people together.' In fact, the attack galvanised so much local support for the garden, there is now talk of starting Turramurra's second community garden. 'We have a waiting list of gardeners who want to join up. We just need more plots,' says John. 'The secret of a community garden is finding a core group of people who are dedicated and determined to make it a success. Our core team has shown that with a little support and cooperation a community garden can be one of the most inspiring places to spend your time.'

I've seen how the social and political life of a community garden is a microcosm of the health of our broader community. So many of the challenges we face as a society require communication, consultation, cooperation, acceptance and generosity. A garden can teach us all these things. The power of gardens lies in the unexpected ways they can bring out the best in us.

All we need to do is slow down occasionally and smell the roses.

How to:

SAVE SEEDS

Sue Dailey (opposite) is a big believer in seed-saving. It not only saves money but ensures you can enjoy your best crops again and again.

Seeds need to be stored in a cool, dry place. Humidity and warmth shorten a seed's shelf-life. A refrigerator is generally the best place to store them.

Keep seed packets in plastic food-storage bags, plastic film canisters or Mason jars with tight-fitting lids.

Store each year's seeds together and date them. This is important since most seeds last about three years.

When you're ready to plant, remove the seed containers from the refrigerator and keep them closed until the seeds warm to room temperature. Otherwise, moisture in the air will condense on the seeds, causing them to clump together.

If you're gathering and saving seeds from your own plants, spread the seeds on newspaper and let them air-dry for about a week.

If you're collecting tomato seeds, soak the seeds in a dish in some water until they begin fermenting. After three days, rinse thoroughly and spread on printer paper (Sue says seeds stick to paper towel). Wait until they are dry and then store them on paper in a jar in the fridge.

Write seed names on the paper so there's no mix-up. Pack the air-dried seeds in small paper packets or envelopes, and label with plant name, date, and other pertinent information.

Remember, if you want to save your own seeds, you'll need to plant open-pollinated varieties. They'll come back true; hybrids won't.

How to:

SET UP A COMMUNITY GARDEN

What do you need to get started?

- a piece of land (and permission to use it)

- six or more hours of sunshine on at least part of the land

- a source of water

- funding source (plot rental fees, sponsorship)

- materials: tools (and a safe place to keep them), soil, compost, fertilisers, edging or fencing material, and plants or seeds

- an organisational approach and a plot plan

- someone knowledgeable about gardening

- people to do the gardening

- a formal or informal management team

- a good communication strategy (website, regular email updates, newsletters, etc).

See the Bibliography for further reading.

AVOCADO

When to plant?
Hot humid climate: Year-round
Hot dry climate: November–March
Cool temperate climate: December–March for certain varieties

What to grow? Waldena and Hazzard varieties in Tropics; Pinkerton, Rincon and Wurtz in sub-tropics and Bacon in cool climate.

Where to grow? In garden or pots.

I like . . . excellent drainage.

I don't like . . . wet feet.

Feed me . . . a complete organic fertiliser, with a bit of extra potash, and gypsum in the spring.

Give me a drink . . . watering me is important. Top me up during the heat of the day.

CANNELLINI BEANS

When to plant?
Hot humid climate: Not suitable
Hot dry climate: April–July
Cool temperate climate: March–June

What to grow: Seed.

Where to grow: Plant where they will grow at a depth three times the diameter of the seed.

I like . . . well-draining soil

I don't like . . . wind. May require staking.

Feed me . . . no need for additional fertiliser, other than manure and compost at planting.

Give me a drink . . . once a week, increasing to twice a week in the hot weather.

PECANS

When to plant?
Hot humid climate: Not suitable
Hot dry climate: June–October
Cool temperate: climate Year-round

What to grow? Trees, which will grow several metres. Some varieties self-pollinate. Good for community garden with acreage.

Where to grow? Northern New South Wales or Southern Queensland. Slow growing. Crops after 5 years.

I like . . . winter chill and then warm conditions with plenty of water.

I don't like . . . water-logged soil.

Feed me . . . a complete pecan-tree fertiliser (with zinc) in late winter.

Give me a drink . . . regularly, especially as fruit are setting.

When to plant? Hot humid climate: Year-round
Hot dry climate: Not suitable
Cool temperate climate: Not suitable

What to grow? Bananas are highly regulated due to diseases and you need a permit to plant or transplant one.

Where to grow? Warm, frost-free, coastal climates.

I like . . . well-composted soil.

I don't like . . . the cold.

Feed me . . . a bucketful of manure and fertiliser four times a year.

Give me a drink . . . regularly – I am very thirsty.

BANANAS

When to plant? Hot humid climate: Not suitable
Hot dry climate: June–July
Cool temperate climate: Year-round

What to grow? Tree bare-footed and dormant.

Where to grow? Cool climates, especially in the mountains of Tasmania and Victoria.

I like . . . sunny spots.

I don't like . . . heat.

Feed me . . . in spring and autumn with organic manures and compost.

Give me a drink . . . I need a steady water supply.

APPLES

When to plant?
Hot humid climate: Can tolerate humidity but summer coastal rain will cause figs to split
Hot dry climate: Year-round
Cool temperate climate: December–April

What to grow? Small sapling.

Where to grow? Hot dry climate. Will grow in large pots.

I like . . . compost-rich, slightly acidic soil.

I don't like . . . harsh wind.

Feed me . . . avoid nitrogen-rich fertilisers or you'll get too much leaf and not much fruit.

Give me a drink . . . I like well-drained soil. Don't overwater me or the fruit will split.

FIGS

Mark's salmon sashimi with avocado dip

Serves 4 as an entree

My husband, Mark, and I spend many Sunday afternoons listening to the brilliant harpist Jake Meadows and his band The Myall High Club play at the oh-so-cool LL Wine and Dine in Kings Cross. This is Mark's version of the delicious entree we always start our meal with.

200 g sashimi-grade salmon, diced
1 teaspoon sesame oil
2 tablespoons lemon juice
1 tablespoon Japanese mayonnaise
¼ teaspoon Sriracha chilli sauce
½ avocado, finely diced
salt and freshly ground black pepper
¼ cup (60 g) creme fraiche
2 tablespoons fish roe
olive oil, to drizzle
lavosh or similar crackers, to serve

Oil an 8 cm × 5 cm ring mould and place it on a serving plate.

In a non-reactive bowl, gently toss the salmon with the sesame oil and 1 tablespoon of lemon juice. Place the salmon mixture in the egg ring.

Mix the mayonnaise with the chilli sauce. Toss the diced avocado with the remaining lemon juice, and spoon it over the salmon mixture, then spread over the chilli mayo. Add a sprinkling of salt and a crack of pepper. Top with the creme fraiche and fish roe and a swirl of olive oil.

Gently lift off the ring mould. Serve with crackers on the side.

Spanish garlic prawns

Serves 4 as part of a platter

Most of my food inspiration comes from my travels. You'll find this dish at nearly every tapas bar in Barcelona. I love soaking up the garlicky oil with some bread.

⅓ cup (80 ml) olive oil
1 red capsicum (pepper), finely diced
6 cloves garlic, thinly sliced
1 teaspoon hot Spanish paprika
1 kg peeled raw (green) prawns, tails intact
salt and freshly ground black pepper
small handful flat-leaf parsley leaves, finely chopped
bread, to serve

Heat the olive oil in a large heavy-based saucepan over medium heat. Add the capsicum and cook for 10 minutes or until soft. Add the garlic, paprika and prawns and fry for 5–8 minutes or until the prawns turn pink. Season to taste.

Toss through the parsley and serve with bread.

Herb-crusted lamb racks with smashed cannellini beans

Serves 6–8

Lamb racks can be expensive, but there is no better cut to show off the flavour of sweet new-season lamb. To make it go further, I serve the lamb with smashed cannellini beans and a few other sides, such as the Roast pumpkin with maple syrup and crispy sage (see page 202).

2 × French-trimmed lamb racks (8 cutlets each)

salt and freshly ground black pepper

1 teaspoon dijon mustard

3 slices sourdough, rye or wholemeal bread

1 clove garlic, finely chopped

1 tablespoon chopped rosemary

1 tablespoon chopped flat-leaf parsley

1 tablespoon chopped sage

1 tablespoon chopped thyme

1 tablespoon finely grated orange zest

juice of 1 orange

2 tablespoons grated parmesan

⅓ cup (80 ml) olive oil, plus extra to drizzle

SMASHED CANNELLINI BEANS

1 × 400 g tin cannellini beans, drained and rinsed

2 cups (500 ml) chicken stock

salt and freshly ground black pepper

olive oil, to drizzle

Preheat the oven to 200°C fan-forced (220°C conventional).

Rub the lamb racks with salt and pepper to taste and the mustard. Set aside on a baking tray with bones facing up, interlocked.

Place the bread in a food processor and blitz to coarse crumbs. In a large mixing bowl, combine the breadcrumbs, garlic, herbs, orange zest and juice, parmesan, olive oil and salt and pepper to taste. Cover the lamb racks with spoonfuls of the stuffing, pressing down firmly with your fingers. Drizzle a little more olive oil over the top.

Roast the lamb for 35–40 minutes (for medium–rare).

Remove from the oven, cover loosely with foil and rest for 10 minutes, then carve into cutlets.

Meanwhile, place the cannellini beans and chicken stock in a small saucepan and bring to rapid simmer. Cook for 10 minutes until the beans are very soft. Smash in the saucepan using a fork, creating a textured mash. Season with salt and pepper.

To serve, place some smashed cannellini beans in a serving dish, drizzle with a little olive oil and top with two carved lamb cutlets.

162

Spiced apple crumble cake

Serves 10

The Turramurra gardeners are excellent bakers. Their Saturday morning teas have already become legendary. I love a cake that uses fresh fruit. Here, the apple is part of the cake's spicy crumble topping.

250 g unsalted butter, softened

250 g caster sugar

4 large eggs

1⅔ cups (250 g) self-raising flour

1 tablespoon finely grated orange zest

1 tablespoon orange juice

1 teaspoon vanilla extract

cream or custard, to serve

CRUMBLE TOPPING

⅓ cup (50 g) plain flour

40 g unsalted butter, softened

40 g brown sugar

½ teaspoon ground cardamom

½ teaspoon ground ginger

½ teaspoon ground cinnamon

2 green apples, finely diced

1 tablespoon caster sugar

Preheat the oven to 180°C fan-forced (200°C conventional). Butter and line a 20 cm springform cake tin.

Using an electric mixer, cream the butter and sugar for about 8 minutes, scraping down the sides, until light and airy. Add one egg at a time, beating well after each addition, until well incorporated. Add the flour and orange zest and beat well, then add the orange juice and vanilla extract. Transfer the batter into the prepared tin.

To make the crumble, rub the flour, butter, brown sugar and spices until the mixture resembles coarse sand. Add the apple and mix well. Spread the topping over the batter and sprinkle evenly with the caster sugar.

Bake for 45–50 minutes until the cake springs back when lightly touched.

Allow to cool for a few minutes in the tin, then carefully remove and cool on a rack.

Serve either cool or warmed with a little cream or custard.

Ingrid's scones with jam

Makes about 12

My friend Ingrid Weir writes a beautiful photography blog called The Old School Master's House (theoldschoolmastershouse.com). I can spend hours lost in her images and evocative prose. This recipe is inspired by one she found in an old Country Women's Association cookbook during her travels. Rhubarb jam is the perfect accompaniment. I always get mine from Tim Petersen's famous Café DOV in Potts Point, Sydney.

40 g unsalted butter
1½ cups (375 ml) milk
3 cups (450 g) self-raising flour, plus extra for dusting
1 tablespoon icing sugar
good pinch of salt
Jam and thickened cream, to serve

Preheat the oven to 250°C and lightly grease a baking sheet.

Melt the butter in half of the milk; you can do this in a large mug in the microwave. Add the melted butter milk to the rest of the milk.

Sift the flour, icing sugar and salt together into a bowl. Make a well in the centre and pour in the milk mixture. Using a fork, gently incorporate the milk mixture into the flour. The mix should be quite moist.

Turn the dough onto a lightly floured bench. Press together, being careful not to overwork the dough or you'll end up with chewy scones.

Cut into rounds and place the scones on the prepared baking sheet. Bake until the tops are golden brown, about 15 minutes.

Serve warm with jam and thickened cream.

Lavender shortbread hearts

Makes 24

It's important to find some culinary lavender for this recipe, not sprigs from the roadside, which could have been sprayed with pesticides. The Turramurra garden is full of organic culinary lavender, which I dried myself and used for this recipe.

1½ cups (225 g) plain flour, plus extra for dusting
115 g rice flour
1½ tablespoons dried culinary lavender
115 g caster sugar, plus extra to sprinkle
250 g unsalted butter, softened and chopped

Preheat the oven to 160°C fan-forced (180°C conventional) and line two baking sheets with baking paper.

Sift the flours together into a bowl and add the lavender and sugar. Rub in the butter and knead into a smooth dough. Shape into a disc, then cover with plastic film and chill in the fridge for 15 minutes.

Turn the dough out onto a floured surface and roll out to 1 cm thickness. Cut out heart shapes. Prick with a fork and sprinkle with the extra caster sugar.

Place on the prepared baking sheet and bake for 35–45 minutes until just beginning to colour around the edges. Cool on a rack.

Banoffee pie

Serves 8

Not satisfied with small-scale urban farming, I've started taking tours of the rooftop farms of New York (see theediblebalcony.com.au for more info). There are several in Brooklyn and Long Island – some 2.5 acres in size. We stay at the glamorous Wythe Hotel in Williamsburg, whose restaurant does a banoffee pie that always leaves tour participants in raptures.

300 ml thickened cream

5 ripe bananas, sliced

chocolate shavings, to decorate

CRUMB BASE

250 g digestive biscuits

100 g pecans

1 teaspoon grated lemon zest

220 g unsalted butter, melted

SALTED TOFFEE SAUCE

200 g caster sugar

80 g butter, chopped

½ cup (125 ml) pouring cream

½ teaspoon salt flakes

To make the crumb base, process the biscuits, pecans and lemon zest in a food processor, then add the melted butter and pulse until combined. Press the mixture into the base of a pie dish, 24 cm in diameter and 5 cm deep. Chill in the fridge for 3 hours or overnight.

For the salted toffee sauce, place the sugar and 50 ml of water in a small heavy-based saucepan. Stir over medium heat until the sugar dissolves, then bring to the boil until the syrup becomes a deep amber colour, 6–8 minutes. Carefully add the butter, cream and salt, and stir until combined. Pour the sauce over the crumb base and chill in the fridge for 1 hour.

Whip the cream until soft peaks form. Arrange some sliced banana on top of the toffee, then top with cream, more sliced banana and chocolate shavings. Serve immediately.

Fitzroy Community Garden

Rebuilding lives

My visits to the Turramurra community garden have shown me the incredibly deep bonds neighbours can develop just from gardening together. Toiling the earth in shared communion can seemingly add meaning and purpose to anyone's life. Or can it? I'm in the gritty inner-city suburbs of Melbourne – a long way from gentrified Turramurra. I'm here to explore a unique gardening experiment with the odds stacked very much against it.

The taxi drops me off on the corner of Napier and Gertrude Streets near the Fitzroy Community Garden. It's lunchtime and the street is bustling with shoppers, young mothers and huddles of self-consciously casual students mulling over their lattes. It is hard to imagine that this hipsterville enclave encircles one of Melbourne's most socially disadvantaged housing areas.

The Atherton Gardens public housing estate dominates the skyline. Its four towers, each twenty storeys high, rise ominously from the centre of 8 acres of parkland on Napier Street. As I look at these Dickensian concrete structures I can't imagine anyone calling them home, yet approximately 1800 people do.

Sitting incongruously in the shadow of the towers, surrounded by cyclone fencing, is the vegetable garden I've come to visit. Its lush green contents contrast starkly with the hard greyness of the housing estate. While the towers are cold and unyielding, the vegetable garden beckons me to come inside.

Towers of disadvantage

In the 1960s and 70s, when the Atherton Gardens Estate was built, the Victorian Government trumpeted high-rise towers as the miracle housing solution for low-income families. In total, twenty-one public housing towers went up across Melbourne, in Fitzroy, Richmond, South Melbourne and Carlton. Many critics, however, argued that these 'suburbs in the sky' would hardly be an improvement on what they replaced – the hundreds of 'slum' dwellings demolished to build them. And in reality many of the homes they replaced were not slums at all. They may have been in a state of disrepair, but many had been renovated by newly arrived immigrants who had installed plumbing and made other improvements. Once their properties were earmarked for demolition, many of these residents never returned to the area.

The program was eventually abandoned when local resistance to building the towers became too loud to ignore. The social planners had got it wrong. The years of disadvantage, unemployment, poverty and illness had not been eradicated; they had just been centralised into vertical ghettoes. The Atherton Gardens Estate became a trouble spot for crime and domestic violence. The statistics have become staggering. Each year between 2007 and 2012, Victoria Police and emergency services reported an average 739 attendances at the estate, the equivalent of almost one call-out a year for each of the 798 apartments. To make living conditions worse, some of the buildings have been poorly maintained over the years, adding to the general sense of decay and despondency.

Authorities have long searched for solutions to this discontent. What could possibly knit these towers of disadvantage into a community?

A place to heal

Many residents who settled into the Atherton Gardens Estate shared an experience of trauma. As refugees or newly arrived immigrants they had left their homes or lost their homes, left their families or lost their families. Now they found themselves far away from their fields and farms, villages and townships, living in four concrete towers with hundreds of other displaced arrivals.

Communicating with neighbours was difficult. At least twelve different languages were spoken amongst the multicultural residents, including Turkish, Arabic, Cantonese, Mandarin, Dari, Farsi, Greek, Macedonian, Pashto, Vietnamese and Somali. With language such a barrier, how could friendships and trust be established?

It was in the estate's surrounding parkland that an idea began taking shape. Many residents had complained it was difficult to buy the traditional herbs and vegetables they were used to cooking with, and that if they *could* find some of these ingredients in the local markets they were often too expensive for them. Growing their own food had been part of their old life – but could it be part of their new one as well? Authorities believed so.

In 1981, work began on converting and extending an existing seating area behind the towers into a 200 square metre community garden. Building work stopped and started as funding came and then dried up. Eventually several raised beds were built and divided into plots that residents could rent for a small annual fee.

Residents watched the building works over the years with a mix of interest and suspicion. They had grown sceptical of councils and governments making promises they never delivered. But behind the scenes there was a group of garden volunteers determined that the new Fitzroy Community Garden was going to have a lasting impact.

Building the garden

Cultivating Community is a Melbourne-based not-for-profit charity that helps organisations grow food for families on low incomes. It has been around in various guises since the late 1990s, initially specialising in helping create and support community gardens for tenants in public housing estates. They now manage nineteen public housing gardens and in the past decade they have expanded their work to include supporting school gardens, and running composting and food waste programmes.

The Fitzroy Community Garden became a passion for Cultivating Community when it was given a State Government grant to take over the running of it in 2003. The project certainly had its particular challenges. The numerous language groups amongst the estate's residents made communication very difficult. Dozens of letterbox drops needed to be organised through translators and interpreters to drum up interest in the new garden. Still many residents were reluctant to be coaxed out of their tiny apartments.

Sharelle Polack from Cultivating Community tells me that threats and violence on the estate were a significant barrier. Many tenants had come from countries ravaged by war and conflict and they still carried the physical as well as emotional scars. Others were elderly with a range of health issues. They weren't sure they'd be safe in this new garden.

A core group of motivated residents began convincing them otherwise. They believed the garden would be a much-needed circuit breaker. It would be a space where everyone would be able to relax with their families, meet their neighbours, make some friends, grow some food or just be with others.

To safeguard tenant security, the garden was fenced off from the surrounding parklands and apartments with a locked gate. This hopefully would reduce theft and vandalism and allow residents to leave their belongings and tools in the garden.

The garden beds were divided into individual plots with two shared communal plots. Wide paths were built between the beds to allow for easy disability access. All participating residents agreed to follow some gardening guidelines. They could grow anything they wanted as long as organic principles were used – no harmful herbicides or insecticides to manage pests, and no chemical-based fertilisers. Soil health in the beds would be critical to high productivity so plans were put in place for a four-bay, green-waste composting system and two Aerobins were added to process food waste. A Cultivating Community support worker was assigned to manage the garden for two hours a week to ensure it was well maintained, clean and safe.

The ground work had been laid – but would it be enough to entice the residents?

> Many residents were reluctant to be coaxed out of their tiny apartments.

The plot thickens

When I visit on a weekday afternoon in late summer, the garden is awash with colour. The gardeners are hard at work, crouching, heads buried deep in the shrubs and bushes. Several Sudanese residents in their traditional, brightly patterned robes and head-dresses, an elderly Chinese gentleman and two young Vietnamese women are working in their plots. There is chatter and laughter and a sense of common purpose.

The diversity of produce under cultivation is breathtaking. The Vietnamese gardeners are harvesting armfuls of Vietnamese mint, parsley, watercress, chillies and lettuces. They're going to use the ingredients to make a fresh salad with a tangy dressing for their lunch. In other plots there are sweet potatoes, cucumbers, pumpkins, kale, cabbages, more chillies and more herbs and greens.

Two Sudanese women are keen to show me their end-of-season eggplants, chillies, spinach, chives and thriving mint bushes. When I ask why they grow so much mint, Amelia Omebi and Sadeira Oman (opposite) tell me they use it to make hot, sweet mint tea, a traditional refreshment in their homeland. They put dried mint leaves, sometimes with a crushed cardamom pod, in a teapot, top it up with hot water and stir in some sugar or honey. Having the mint in their plot and knowing they can pick it for fresh tea whenever they want eases their homesickness.

Wars in Northern Sudan forced them both to flee their home ten or so years ago. They say it's taken them a long time to settle into Australian life and having the garden has made the transition easier. 'I worked on a farm growing corn in Sudan so I know how to grow,' says Sadeira. 'But I do need help to know what to grow in this climate.' When she first started her plot she says she would overwater her crops and drown them. 'Of course it is much drier in Sudan,' she explains, laughing at her earlier inexperience. With advice from the Asian gardeners Sadeira is also growing tatsoi (a small-leafed Chinese cabbage) and some Asian basil. 'I don't know how to cook with them but they give me recipes to try,' she says.

Sadeira spends about an hour in her plot every day watering and managing pests. An annoying mouse has been gnawing at her basil so she plans to put in more stakes and some stronger netting around her crops to protect them. She also enjoys the social aspect of gardening. It has given her the opportunity to chat to neighbours she used to pass for years in the building without talking to.

'I like meeting people and sharing the food I grow and getting new recipes to try,' she says, her eyes lighting up. She shares her apartment with her three sons and a daughter, who come and go depending on their employment situation. 'It is hard for them to find work,' says Sadeira. Her daughter is studying environmental studies at university, she tells me proudly. 'I hope she can get a good job.'

Sadeira especially loves the sense of self-sufficiency the garden provides her with. She says she comes from a very proud culture. 'We want to give to Australia, not take from it,' she explains. 'The garden shows people what we can do for ourselves. We want to work hard.'

Before I leave she snips off a small stem from a bush in her plot with tiny yellow-white flowers. 'Try this,' she says. 'It is medicine.' Sadeira tells me the herb is called rue and it is used in Sudan to ease stomach pain and cramps. It's added to boiled milk and drunk as a tea. I take a bite and chew. It has a sweet taste and I can immediately feel my tongue numbing slightly. Powerful medicinal herbal knowledge clearly resides in her culture.

Some of the ingredients from Sadeira's garden will be used for our brick-oven-baked garden lunch today and I leave her to pick a few herbs and chillies. I can't wait to taste them.

The shared hearth

An enticing aroma of burning charcoal is coming from the garden's brick oven. The oven stands almost 3 metres high, like a huge, curved, ochre-coloured igloo. Volunteer baker Rob Di Leva (left) is big and broad and is building up a sweat as he stokes the fire, moving the embers across the oven floor so the heat is evenly distributed. Despite his apparent expertise and ease around outdoor ovens, Rob tells me he is new to baking and is actually a trained physiotherapist.

'When I heard there was an original Alan Scott-built brick oven in this garden I couldn't keep away,' says Rob in awe. 'I'm here cooking bread and pizza most weeks to hone my skills and to give the residents a few tips as well.' Blacksmith Alan Scott, Rob tells me, is the godfather of brick ovens – so famous in fact that his death in 2009 garnered a full-page obituary in the *The New York Times*. Although he was born in the Melbourne suburb of Toorak, most of the 4000 ovens Alan built or inspired others to build are scattered throughout the world, from Alaska to Venezuela to South Africa. So the existence of one right here in the humble Fitzroy Community Garden is – I now agree with Rob – quite extraordinary.

Put it down to fortuitous timing. Cultivating Community contacted Alan in the United States, where he was based, for advice about how to build one of his ovens. The call for help coincided with Alan returning to Australia due to ill-health and he was able to personally oversee the construction of the oven during a three-day workshop in the garden in March 2005. The estate residents now had a veggie garden and a stylish wood-fired oven built by the world's most famous oven builder. They must have been pinching themselves.

Alan Scott would have been greatly moved by the achievement as well. He had given a disadvantaged community an open hearth where they could cook and share meals together, surrounded by a garden bursting with produce they had grown themselves.

Through his Californian-based company, Ovencrafters, and the book he co-authored, *The Bread Builders: Hearth Loaves and Masonry Ovens,* Alan Scott reignited a worldwide interest in artisanal backyard baking and its ability to bring communities together. He perfected the ancient art of brick oven-building by using high-grade bricks, modern insulation and even ceramic blankets. The ovens are relatively straightforward to operate. It's just a case of burning some wood on the hearth floor, then sweeping away the ashes and baking food in the remaining radiant heat. Temperatures can reach up to 400°C in these ovens, giving bread that moist crumb and crisp crust that enthusiasts get giddy over (for 'enthusiasts' insert 'Indira').

For our garden lunch today, Rob has made some yeasty pizza dough and is using a mixture of bought and garden-grown ingredients for toppings, and fillings for his moreish calzone. He skilfully slides each pizza into the oven using his baker's wooden 'peel' or paddle.

Hungry hordes are gathering in the garden kitchen. The table is being set for a feast. There are more than seven nationalities represented here. Few things have the power to bring people together the way food has.

Everything that comes out of the oven is scented with charcoal and wood smoke. The pizza crusts are crisp, the dough chewy and Sadeira's garden chillies and capsicums have taken on a charred, earthy sweetness. The silence as we eat is an indication of our enjoyment.

I could eat like this every day. Cooking in wood-fired ovens with garden-fresh produce is how our ancestors sustained themselves. There is something very primal about the experience of sharing food over a fire. It taps deep into our DNA. When we can grow and cook our food in the open under the trees we can become part of nature again. On days like today even people with very little would feel they have everything they've ever wished for.

Giving hope

It has now been more than thirty years since the Fitzroy Community Garden was first conceived. It has expanded and had many building additions, including compost bins, a shed, and of course the communal kitchen and outdoor brick oven. The number of garden plots has increased to seventy-one. Everything seems to be flourishing.

This is a community that is attempting to create its own future.

As I fly back to Sydney that evening I watch a story on the inflight news about another riot at the Manus Island Detention Centre. Our treatment of vulnerable people can't be in stronger contrast to what I have seen today. I hope we'll soon realise that refugee policy without kindness and compassion will never work. Why build prisons when we can build gardens?

How to:

COMPOST

The Fitzroy Community Garden uses a three-bin composting system that produces nutritious compost. Here are a few tips from the gardeners about making healthy compost.

Compost that is too wet will not allow enough air for aerobic microbes (the good ones) to survive, so the anaerobic ones (the bad ones) take over. They can produce foul-smelling gases. To fix this add some 'brown' dry material, such as straw, sawdust, dried leaves or old dried lawn clippings. You can also add shredded newspaper (not glossy printed materials as they contain toxic inks) and kitchen paper towels – as long as they do not contain oil, liquid from meat/dairy products or anything cooked, such as soup.

Turn your compost when adding layers of the 'brown' dry materials to the existing compost. Turn it at least two or three times a week.

The compost should look like a wet blanket, not dripping wet and not bone-dry. This will be the perfect condition for the worms and bacteria to break down the compost.

Ensure your compost bin can drain freely. Even better, cover your compost to prevent rain entering.

If your compost is too dry, add water and more 'green materials', such as fruit and vegetable scraps and garden prunings.

If your bin is attracting vinegar flies, sprinkle it with lime.

CAPSICUM

When to plant?
Hot humid climate: May–July
Hot dry climate: November–April
Cool temperate climate: October–December

What to grow? Can be direct planted from seed or seedling.

Where to grow? Can grow in garden bed or pots but need to be staked.

I like . . . sun.

I don't like . . . very hot weather or flowers will drop. Provide some shade.

Feed me . . . fortnightly with a low-nitrogen liquid fertiliser.

Give me a drink . . . regularly.

ZUCCHINI

When to plant?
Hot humid climate: January–March; August–December
Hot dry climate: September–December
Cool temperate climate: October–December

What to grow? Wide variety from seed including blackjack and Lebanese.

Where to grow? In beds or large containers.

I like . . . full sun.

I don't like . . . humidity can cause fungal diseases such as powdery mildew.

Feed me . . . apply Dynamic Lifter around my base each month.

Give me a drink . . . I need a steady water supply.

PUMPKIN

When to plant?
Hot humid climate: April–July
Hot dry climate: September–February
Cool temperate climate: September–December

What to grow? From seed in pots or beds. Can be started indoors or in greenhouses in cool climates.

Where to grow? In full sun.

I like . . . open well-drained soil with lots of compost.

I don't like . . . overcrowding. Prone to mildew.

Feed me . . . light organic water-soluble applications every three to four weeks.

Give me a drink . . . only on surface not leaves.

KALE

When to plant?
Hot humid climate: June–July
Hot dry climate: March–July
Cool temperate climate: May–June

What to grow? From seed into
seed trays.

Where to grow? Plant out seedlings into
containers and beds.

I like . . . frost – it improves flavour.

I don't like . . . growing in the same bed
as tomatoes or beans.

Feed me . . . a well-composted soil with
manure when first planted.

Give me a drink . . . regularly to keep
leaves sweet.

TURMERIC

When to plant?
Hot humid climate: March–November
Hot dry climate: Not suitable
Cool temperate climate: Not suitable

What to grow? Can use shop-bought
turmeric to grow own plants.

Where to grow? In warm climates but
will die down in winter.

I like . . . heat and moisture.

I don't like . . . frosts.

Feed me . . . Dynamic Lifter or other
organic fertiliser during growing months.

Give me a drink . . . keep me
well-watered.

Guacamole

Serves 6

This guacamole is best made just before you're about to serve it, so the avocado does not discolour. I like my guacamole chunky rather than mashed. It gives the dip a better texture – and doesn't remind me of baby food!

2 tomatoes, finely diced
2 avocados, diced
1 small red onion, finely diced
large handful coriander leaves
2 tablespoons lime juice
1 small red chilli, seeded and finely chopped
salt and freshly ground black pepper
corn chips, to serve

Toss the tomato, avocado, onion, coriander, lime juice and chilli together gently in a bowl. Season well with salt and pepper.

Serve with corn chips to the side.

Stuffed dates

Makes 20

You're not going to believe how delicious these stuffed dates are. Warm, sweet and tangy, and all wrapped up into a perfect parcel with a bit of crisp prosciutto. Try to get the best medjool date variety you can afford. It will make all the difference.

20 fresh medjool dates
20 smoked almonds
200 g blue cheese, chopped into 20 pieces
200 g prosciutto, sliced into 20 lengths
2 tablespoons pistachios, finely chopped

Preheat the oven to 180°C fan-forced (200°C conventional) and line a baking tray with baking paper.

Make an incision in the dates lengthways and remove the stones. Place an almond and a piece of blue cheese inside. Wrap a length of prosciutto around each date and secure with a toothpick.

Bake for 10–15 minutes or until the prosciutto crisps up. Sprinkle with chopped pistachios and serve.

Zucchini soup with zucchini flowers

Serves 4 as a main or 6 as an entree

This is a lovely elegant soup to whip up in summer when zucchini are plentiful. If you want to add a little extra richness, finish off with a dollop of creme fraiche in each bowl.

2 tablespoons olive oil
1 onion, finely chopped
4 cloves garlic, finely chopped
½ red bird's-eye chilli, seeded and finely diced
1 kg zucchini (courgettes), trimmed, cut lengthways and diced
1 desiree potato, peeled and finely diced
1 litre chicken stock or vegetable stock
salt and freshly ground black pepper
4 zucchini (courgette) flowers
grated parmesan, to serve

Heat the olive oil in a heavy-based saucepan over medium heat and fry the onion for 10 minutes or until soft and golden. Add the garlic and chilli and cook for 1 minute until fragrant. Add the zucchini and potato, then cover with the lid and cook over low heat for 12–15 minutes until very soft. Add the stock and season with salt and pepper to taste. Cook for a further 5 minutes. Using a hand blender, blitz the soup until smooth.

Remove the bitter yellow stamen from the centre of each zucchini flower and slice the flowers thinly.

Ladle the soup into bowls and top with grated parmesan and zucchini flowers. Serve immediately.

Kale, prosciutto and blue cheese tart

Serves 8

So many food trends come and go. Right now kale is having its moment in the culinary limelight and I hope it never goes out of fashion. It is so versatile and nutritious. I like serving a wedge of this tart with a bitter leaf salad, which helps to cut through the richness.

1 pre-rolled butter puff pastry sheet, thawed

2 tablespoons thyme leaves

1 egg, beaten

1 large bunch kale, finely chopped

1 tablespoon olive oil

1 onion, thinly sliced

1 teaspoon brown mustard seeds

salt and freshly ground black pepper

small handful chopped flat-leaf parsley

180 g blue cheese, chopped

2 eggs (extra)

4 egg yolks

200 ml pouring cream

200 g sour cream

200 g prosciutto (about 4 strips)

Preheat the oven to 180°C fan-forced (200°C conventional).

Sprinkle the pastry sheet with the thyme leaves. Roll it out to fit a pie dish 27 cm in diameter and 5 cm deep. Prick the base all over with a fork. Line with baking paper and fill with baking beans or rice, then blind-bake for 10–12 minutes or until lightly golden. Remove from the oven and remove the paper and baking beans. Brush the base with the beaten egg, return to the oven and bake for 6 minutes until golden and crisp.

Reduce the oven temperature to 150°C.

Place the kale in a large heavy-based saucepan over medium heat. Place a lid on top and allow to soften and wilt for 15–20 minutes.

Heat the olive oil in a frying pan over medium heat and add the onion. Fry for 4–5 minutes until soft. Add the kale and mustard seeds and cook for a further minute. Season with salt and pepper to taste. Spread the kale mix over the tart case, then sprinkle over the parsley and scatter over the blue cheese.

In a bowl, whisk the eggs, yolks, cream and sour cream. Season with salt and pepper to taste, then pour into the tart case. Place the prosciutto strips on top.

Bake for 40–50 minutes or until light golden and just set with a slight wobble.

Leave to stand for 10 minutes, then serve.

North African lamb soup

Serves 4

Fitzroy Community Gardener Sadeira says there are versions of this lamb dish all throughout her region of North Africa. It is a perfect winter warmer, with the lemon and the sweet spices giving it a unique flavour.

1 tablespoon vegetable oil, or as needed
4 lamb shanks, French-trimmed
salt
2 red onions, finely chopped
1½ tablespoons tomato paste (puree)
¼ cup (60 ml) lemon juice
1 teaspoon chilli flakes
1 teaspoon ground turmeric
1 teaspoon ground cinnamon
pinch of saffron threads
1 litre chicken stock, or as needed
12 small new potatoes, skin on, halved
4 tomatoes, cut into wedges
1 × 400 g tin chickpeas, drained and rinsed
coriander leaves, to garnish
couscous, to serve

Heat the oil in a casserole over high heat and add the lamb shanks. Season with salt and cook for 10 minutes, turning to brown all sides. Remove the shanks from the casserole and keep warm on a plate loosely covered with foil.

Add the onion to the casserole (some fat should have rendered from the lamb but add another tablespoon of oil if you need to). Add the onion and fry for 5 minutes over medium heat until just beginning to colour. Return the lamb to the casserole. Add the tomato paste, lemon juice, chilli, spices and chicken stock.

Cover with a lid and simmer for 2 hours, adding more stock if it becomes too dry. Add the potatoes and cook for a further 30 minutes, then add the tomato and chickpeas and cook for another 20 minutes or until the lamb is falling off the bone.

Garnish with coriander leaves and serve with couscous.

Crispy whole fish with Thai dressing

Serves 6

This is a Sunday lunch 'wow' dish. Many people are intimidated by cooking a whole fish, but I encourage you to give it a go. The sauce, vegetables and herbs can be pre-prepared and the fish can be quickly fried just before you're ready to eat. Choose a whole fish with clear eyes and shiny skin.

1 × 750 g whole white fish, such as snapper, gutted and scaled

salt

6 cm piece ginger, roughly chopped

1 bulb garlic, cloves chopped

4 red bird's-eye chillies, seeded

100 ml fish sauce

100 ml lime juice

½ cup (130 g) grated palm sugar

vegetable oil, for shallow frying

4 spring onions, sliced

large handful mint leaves

large handful coriander leaves

steamed rice, to serve

Score the fish four or five times on each side through the flesh. Rub all over with salt.

Using a mortar and pestle, pound the ginger, garlic and chilli with a teaspoon of salt to make a rough paste. Stir in the fish sauce, lime juice and palm sugar and 2 tablespoons of water. Simmer the sauce in a small heavy-based saucepan over low heat for 10 minutes or until it becomes syrupy.

Meanwhile, pour the vegetable oil into a large wok or heavy-based frying pan until deep enough to come halfway up the sides of the fish. Heat the oil until hot but not smoking. Carefully lower in the fish and fry on each side for about 5–8 minutes or until cooked; the flesh should be white and opaque. Drain on paper towel.

Arrange the fish on a serving platter. Spoon the sauce over the fish. Garnish with spring onions, mint and coriander. Serve with rice.

Roast pumpkin with maple syrup and crispy sage

Serves 6 as a side

Pumpkin, maple syrup and sage are a match made in heaven—I don't need to say much more really. This dish is a perfect side to a roast or pasta dish and leftovers can be tossed with some spinach leaves for a light salad lunch.

1 kg kent (jap) pumpkin, skin on, sliced into wedges
⅓ cup (80 ml) olive oil
2 tablespoons maple syrup
1 teaspoon ground cinnamon
handful of sage leaves
salt and freshly ground black pepper
2 tablespoons black chia seeds (optional)

Preheat the oven to 200°C fan-forced (220°C conventional)

Place the pumpkin wedges in a bowl. Add the olive oil, maple syrup, cinnamon and sage leaves, then season with salt and pepper and toss well to coat.

Spread out on a baking tray and roast for 30–40 minutes or until the pumpkin is soft and golden. Sprinkle with chia seeds, if you like, and serve.

Baked Greek chicken with olives

Serves 8

Everyone needs a quick chicken bake in their bag of tricks – especially when you just don't have the energy to cook. In this recipe the oven does all the work for you, producing a casserole that is perfect for a packed lunch the next day as well.

750 g small new potatoes, skin on
8 small chicken thighs, skin on
2 teaspoons sweet paprika
¼ cup (60 ml) olive oil
1 tablespoon lemon juice
2 red onions, thickly sliced
1 red capsicum (pepper), seeded and sliced into strips
1 yellow capsicum (pepper), seeded and sliced into strips
4 cloves garlic, thinly sliced
2 tablespoons chopped oregano
salt and freshly ground black pepper
4 ripe tomatoes, chopped
12 black olives
150 g feta, crumbled (optional)
small handful flat-leaf parsley, chopped

Preheat the oven to 200°C fan-forced (220°C conventional)

Place the potatoes in a saucepan of water and bring to the boil. Cook for 5 minutes to par-boil them. Leave to cool slightly, then cut into quarters.

Pat the chicken dry with paper towel, then roughly cut into large chunks and place in a large baking dish. Sprinkle over the paprika, olive oil and lemon juice. Add the potato, onion, capsicum, garlic and oregano, and toss well. Season with salt and pepper.

Bake for 30 minutes, then add the tomatoes and olives, and cook for a further 15 minutes, occasionally basting the chicken with the pan juices.

Remove the chicken from oven and sprinkle with feta, if you like, and chopped parsley. Serve.

Frozen banana and
peanut butter ice-cream

Serves 6

No one can ever believe that just three ingredients can produce this delicious creamy ice-cream. I always keep a stash of over-ripe sliced bananas in my freezer to make this extra-quick treat for the kids.

4 bananas
2 tablespoons milk, if needed
⅓ cup (95 g) crunchy peanut butter

Slice the bananas into rounds, place on a baking tray lined with baking paper and freeze for 2 hours.

Using a blender or food processor, blitz the frozen banana for 10 minutes or until smooth and light, scraping down the sides every so often. Add the milk if the mixture isn't coming together. Add the peanut butter and blitz to combine.

Serve immediately.

Give Peas a Chance

During the past five years as I've explored the food gardens springing up throughout our cities, there is one thing I can say with certainty: No two are alike. Food gardens are as diverse as their gardeners. They are as unique as their locations and as distinctive as their produce.

The motivations for transforming a derelict wedge of urban space into a veggie patch are equally varied. At Sydney's Wayside Chapel the desire was to create a calm space for homeless visitors to learn some gardening and cooking skills and access nutritious, affordable food. At Mesa Verde restaurant's rooftop worm farm the drive was to show businesses the value of reducing your carbon footprint by composting and growing your produce on site. The students at Our Lady of Mount Carmel Catholic Primary School created a food garden where learning was fun, improved their diet and reconnected them with their Indigenous heritage. The Turramurra gardeners wanted to create a sense of togetherness while establishing a green oasis on a blighted stretch of highway. And the residents who rented plots in the Fitzroy Community Garden found a place where they could feel safe and welcomed, and where they could grow the food of their homelands.

As different as they are, what these communities *do* share is a determination not to let a 'rule' or a 'regulation' stop them reimagining their urban spaces. What was green can be green again. Their drive to revitalise their local food systems has been inspiring to document. In an era of increasing citizen apathy, these communities are reasserting their rights over planners and developers. They're taking ownership. Community gardens are democratising our public spaces.

Far from attracting the 'wrong sort of people' I've seen how gardens often attract the 'right sort': people of immense drive and generosity; people who care and are compassionate; people who are gentle and considerate; people who are stewards of the environment.

Cities can be cold, lonely places. We don't see our families much. Our long commute to work trapped in endless traffic isolates us even further. Most of us don't realise it but we're hungry to belong; to give; to contribute to something that matters. Sharing a meal around the hearth enjoying food we've grown together used to be a daily ritual for all of us. Now we come home, microwave a frozen pizza and eat it alone on the couch while we watch a television cooking show. No wonder many of us are miserable.

The gardeners I've come to know have shown me that we can reclaim some of these lost traditions even when we live in cities with little space to grow. The new 'food citizenship' they're part of is a powerful grassroots movement. It's able to activate a complex network of governments, councils, businesses, not-for-profit groups, churches and highly motivated individuals to bring about extraordinary urban transformations.

We are the food we eat. It becomes our flesh and bones, skin and muscle. We walk around with it, in us, on us, every day of our lives. There is no more intimate relationship in our lives than the one we have with food. And the food choices we make affect not only *our* health but the health of our planet.

I hope after reading this book that you can begin picturing those alienating tracts of endless freeways, office towers, tarmac and concrete as places where a seed might take root instead.

And I hope you're the one who plants it.

Bibliography

Long, Graham, *Love Over Hate: Finding Life by the Wayside*. The Slattery Media Group, Melbourne, 2013.

Noffs, Ted, *The Wayside Chapel: A Radical Christian Experiment in Today's World*. Fontana, 1969.

Nowra, Louis. *Kings Cross: A Biography*. UNSW Press, Sydney, 2013.

Pollan, Michael. *Cooked: A Natural History of Transformation*. Penguin Press, New York, 2013.

Purdie, Doug. *Backyard Bees: A Guide for the Beginner Beekeeper*. Murdoch Books, Sydney, 2014.

Scott, Alan and Wing, Daniel, *The Bread Builders: Hearth Loaves and Masonry Ovens*. Chelsea Green Publishing, Vermont, 1999.

Sparrow, Jill and Jeff. *Radical Melbourne: A Secret History*. Vulgar Press, Melbourne, 2001.

INTERNET RESOURCES

The Wayside Chapel Rooftop Garden

thewaysidechapel.com

environastudio.com.au

City of Sydney Green Roof Resource Manual (Environa Studio, 2013): cityofsydney.nsw.gov.au data/assets/pdf_file/0006/109383/Green-roof-resource-manual-full-version.pdf

Bee-keeping:

theurbanbeehive.com.au

Mesa Verde Restaurant Worm Farm

mesaverde.net.au

Food waste:

foodwise.com.au

Worm-farming:

hungrybin.co.nz

tumbleweed.com.au

wormlovers.com.au

BIBLIOGRAPHY

Mount Carmel School Bush-Tucker Garden

olmcwaterloo.catholic.edu.au

Native foods:

atasteofthebush.com.au

Profile on Indigenous native food expert Clarence Slockee:
abc.net.au/gardening/stories/s2810010.htm

Turramurra Lookout Community Garden

tlcgarden.org.au

Starting a community garden:

cityofsydney.nsw.gov.au/community/participation/community-gardens

communitygarden.org.au

homelife.com.au/gardening/features/starting+a+community+garden

Community gardens research:

Hatherly, Janelle, *Community gardens: More than urban green spaces*. Royal Botanic Gardens, Sydney.

Wise, Poppy, *Grow Your Own: The potential values and impacts of residential and community food gardening*. The Australia Institute, 2014. tai.org.au/content/grow-your-own

planning.act.gov.au/tools_resources/research-based-planningdemand_ for_community_ gardens_and_their_benefits

Fitzroy Community Garden

cultivatingcommunity.org.au

The history of Atherton Gardens Estate: museumvictoria.com.au/discoverycentre/infosheets/the-melbourne-story/high-rise-housing-in-melbourne-atherton-gardens-estate-fitzroy

The Nunnawadding Community Gardens: slater.ncg.org.au

Tips on what to grow when

Burke's Backyard fact sheets: burkesbackyard.com.au

The Diggers Club: diggers.com.au

Gardening Australia fact sheets: abc.net.au/gardening/factsheets/fruit_vegetables_herbs

Acknowledgements

'For a seed to achieve its greatest expression, it must come completely undone. The shell cracks, its insides come out and everything changes. To someone who doesn't understand growth, it would look like complete destruction.'

~ *Cynthia Occelli*

Writing a book can be a little like what a seed goes through. You sit at your desk, strip yourself bare (figuratively) and hope inspiration will break out of you like the bursting kernel of a seed. Most of the time nothing happens. You sit there, impotent, immobilised – and spend too much time on Facebook! Then – if you're lucky – the writer's block will give way to a feverish burst of mad typing. Hopefully something is usable. I set my aspirations low. I'm happy with a good paragraph from a morning's work. An illustrative gardening cookbook provides added challenges. There's recipe testing, location shoots, and dozens of people to wrangle.

The first group of collaborators to thank are the gardeners who let me into their lives and entrusted me with their stories. They are the inspiration for this book. I couldn't have crossed the finish line without their generosity and enthusiasm for the project.

From the Wayside Chapel in Kings Cross in Sydney, deepest thanks to Wendy Suma, Bec McKenna, Jen Lee, Bill Suma, Lindsay Morrison, Laura Watts, Sarah Susak, Anna Partridge, Graham Long, Claudia Karvan, David Wenham, Kylie Kwong, Colin Tate, Tone Wheeler and, most importantly, Alan Claremont and all the Wayside garden visitors.

At the Mesa Verde restaurant rooftop worm farm in Melbourne, a huge thank you to Richard Thomas, Kathy Reed, Tim Peach and the staff and gardeners.

At the Our Lady of Mount Carmel Catholic Primary School in Waterloo, Sydney, thank you to teachers Alisha Bourke, Helen Thornborough, headmaster John Farrell and all the gorgeous children in the Garden Club. You have built a beautiful, inclusive school community.

To the inspiring John Dailey and the gardeners at the Turramurra Lookout Community Garden in Sydney, thank you for your time, and delicious morning teas.

And finally to the wonderful gardeners at the Fitzroy Community Garden in Melbourne who have overcome so many hurdles to build their verdant oasis – thank you for sharing your gardening world with me. And thank you to Sharelle Polack and the team at Cultivating Communities for organising our shoot days and acting as translators.

ACKNOWLEDGEMENTS

To my Edible Balcony garden team of supporters – Jon Kingston, Tim Petersen, Scott Monro, Michelle Darlington, Joshi Pitman, Ed Warburton at Greenwall Australia – thank you for making gardening so much fun, and for the champers when it wasn't!

My name may appear on the cover, but don't be fooled. A community of creatives has sweated blood over this book as well.

Fortuitously my photographer and dear friend Alan Benson, who shot my first book, *The Edible Balcony,* agreed to join my circus again. Alan, your enthusiasm and brilliance shines through on every page. I sent you up death-defying ladders, hanging off balconies and rooftops, in the rain and heat, on a desperate dash to the corner store to pick up a forgotten ingredient for a recipe shoot. You're an angel.

A massive thank you to food stylist David Morgan who made cooking and shooting forty dishes in four days seem almost normal. A smile on your face and a smile in your heart, you made every dish look delectable.

Big thank yous to the rest of my fabulous team at Lantern: Katrina O'Brien, Cass Stokes, Emily O'Neill, Alissa Dinallo and my sensational editor, Ariane Durkin. And it wouldn't have happened at all without the foresight and guidance of the indefatigable Julie Gibbs.

Thank you to Jennifer Naughton and Beverley Flower at my agency RGM Artists for their friendship, wisdom and sage advice.

To my husband, Mark FitzGerald, who acted as chief cheerleader, first-draft editor, recipe guinea pig: again I couldn't have attempted another book without your unwavering support. (I told you it would be easier than the first book. OK – I was wrong on that count).

And to you, the reader, thank you for selecting this book from the many thousands and for sharing this precious journey with us.

I'm off to have a cuppa now.

~ *Indira*

Index

LANTERN

UK | USA | Canada | Ireland | Australia
India | New Zealand | South Africa | China

Penguin Books is part of the Penguin Random House group of companies whose addresses can be found at global.penguinrandomhouse.com.

 Penguin
Random House
Australia

First published by Penguin Group (Australia), 2015

10 9 8 7 6 5 4 3 2 1

Text copyright © Indira Naidoo 2015
Photographs copyright © Alan Benson 2015, except page 4 © Doug Williamson 2015

The moral right of the author has been asserted.

All rights reserved. Without limiting the rights under copyright reserved above, no part of this publication may be reproduced, stored in or introduced into a retrieval system, or transmitted, in any form or by any means (electronic, mechanical, photocopying, recording or otherwise), without the prior written permission of both the copyright owner and the above publisher of this book.

Design by Alissa Dinallo and Emily O'Neill © Penguin Group (Australia)
Photography by Alan Benson,
Illustration on page 209 by Indira Naidoo
Food styling by David Morgan

Typeset in ITC Century Light by Post Pre-Press Group, Brisbane, Queensland
Colour separation by Splitting Image Colour Studio, Clayton, Victoria
Printed and bound in China by Toppan Leefung Printing Limited

National Library of Australia
Cataloguing-in-Publication data:

Naidoo, Indira

The edible city

ISBN: 9781921383816 (paperback)

Includes index.

Kitchen gardens.
Community gardens.
Urban gardening.

Benson, Alan (photographer)

635

penguin.com.au/lantern